To my Darling

With all my love (

this day and a happy & heal

Peter

25.xii.09.

DORSET IN WARTIME: THE DIARY OF PHYLLIS WALTHER 1941–1942

Edited by Patricia and Robert Malcolmson

DORSET RECORD SOCIETY

VOLUME 15

2009

Published 2009 Dorset Record Society
Dorset County Museum, Dorchester, Dorset

Typeset in Times New Roman Monotype
and printed by Henry Ling Ltd., The Dorset Press, Dorchester, Dorset
on Chromomat 100 gsm
Cover case bound in Heritage Library Buckram over 3 mm boards.

British Library Cataloguing in Publication Data
Dorset in Wartime, the Diary of Phyllis Walther, 1941–1942
A catalogue record for this book is available from the British Library.

This volume was published with assistance from the Marc Fitch Fund and the
Mansel-Pleydell and Cecil Trust, whose help is gratefully acknowledged.

ISBN

0–900339–15–2
978–0-900339–15–8

Contents

Dorset in Wartime, the Diary of Phyllis Walther, 1941–1942

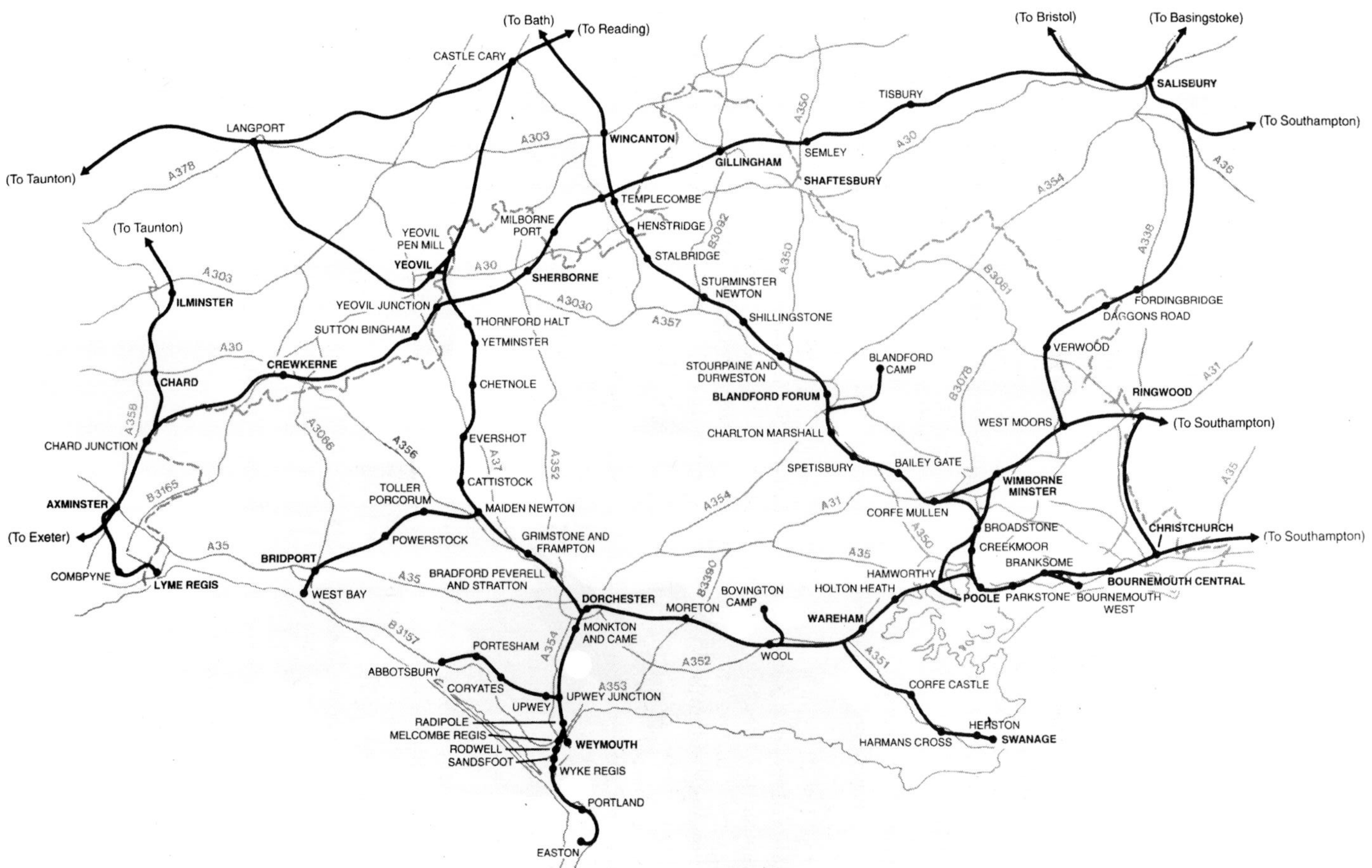

(To Bath)
(To Reading)
(To Bristol)
(To Basingstoke)
SALISBURY
(To Southampton)
CASTLE CARY
LANGPORT
(To Taunton)
WINCANTON
TISBURY
SEMLEY
GILLINGHAM
SHAFTESBURY
TEMPLECOMBE
MILBORNE PORT
YEOVIL PEN MILL
YEOVIL
HENSTRIDGE
STALBRIDGE
(To Taunton)
ILMINSTER
SHERBORNE
YEOVIL JUNCTION
THORNFORD HALT
STURMINSTER NEWTON
SHILLINGSTONE
FORDINGBRIDGE
DAGGONS ROAD
SUTTON BINGHAM
YETMINSTER
VERWOOD
CREWKERNE
CHARD
CHETNOLE
STOURPAINE AND DURWESTON
BLANDFORD CAMP
BLANDFORD FORUM
RINGWOOD
WEST MOORS
(To Southampton)
CHARD JUNCTION
EVERSHOT
CHARLTON MARSHALL
SPETISBURY
BAILEY GATE
CATTISTOCK
WIMBORNE MINSTER
AXMINSTER
TOLLER PORCORUM
MAIDEN NEWTON
CORFE MULLEN
BROADSTONE
CHRISTCHURCH
(To Exeter)
POWERSTOCK
GRIMSTONE AND FRAMPTON
CREEKMOOR
(To Southampton)
BRIDPORT
BRANKSOME
COMBPYNE
LYME REGIS
BRADFORD PEVERELL AND STRATTON
HAMWORTHY
BOURNEMOUTH CENTRAL
WEST BAY
BOVINGTON CAMP
HOLTON HEATH
POOLE
PARKSTONE
BOURNEMOUTH WEST
DORCHESTER
MORETON
WAREHAM
MONKTON AND CAME
PORTESHAM
WOOL
ABBOTSBURY
CORFE CASTLE
CORYATES
UPWEY JUNCTION
UPWEY
RADIPOLE
HERSTON
MELCOMBE REGIS
WEYMOUTH
HARMANS CROSS
SWANAGE
RODWELL
SANDSFOOT
WYKE REGIS
PORTLAND
EASTON
A303
A378
A30
A350
A36
A354
B3092
A3030
A357
A338
B3081
B3078
A31
A358
A3066
A356
A37
A352
B3165
A35
A354
A350
B3390
B3157
A353
A351

Foreword

The first my brother John and I knew of the existence of this diary was a letter from the keeper of the Mass Observation Archive at Sussex University. She had received a request from the Malcolmsons, whose researches had unearthed our Mother's diary, to put us in contact.

It was with a degree of trepidation that we said yes, having seen the 'Housewife 49' television interpretation of Nella Last and the resulting publicity. We met Patricia and Bob and were assured that our Mother's style as a diarist would make this much lower key, in line with her retiring personality. Since then our small involvement, deciphering her handwritten section and putting names to people's initials, has been fascinating. My lasting regret is that my impending birth in September 1942 cut the diary short, or so I assume.

For me, the diary is an incredibly interesting 'snapshot' of my Mother's life and her personality. Her own analysis was that her sheltered upbringing and early education by a governess in the shadow of her 3 sisters, (the eldest, Isabel, being very intelligent; Kitkat, very literary; and a bumptious, extrovert younger sister, Christine), made her embarrassingly encumbered by shyness touched with a degree of guilt at her privileged start. There is no doubt that the years spent in the company of university students, both as one herself reading Botany, and as the efficient keeper of the successful student boarding houses she ran in London, made her views more radical than her family background might suggest. She was still subscribing to the *Guardian Weekly Review* and the *New Statesman* in her 90s as well as having two library books on the go, one fiction and one biography. In her diary she comes over as the capable, industrious, self-reliant and intelligent person that she was.

She was a terrific Mother; life was always fun and active. She coped with the adversity of being a hard-up divorcee in the 1950s stoically. Gardening was always her great passion, and she became a knowledgeable plants-woman. She was to be seen cycling around Swanage well into her 70s with her secateurs in the basket, plying her trade as an expert pruner.

Patricia and Bob Malcolmson are to be thanked for their industrious researches. John and I spent a very pleasant day with them, meandering through Dorset's memory lanes while they got a feel for the places mentioned. Ann Smith of the Dorset Record Society must be commended for the subtlety of her hounding, encouraging me to ask cousins to scour their photo albums for a few replacements for those unfortunately lost to burglars.

Julian Walther

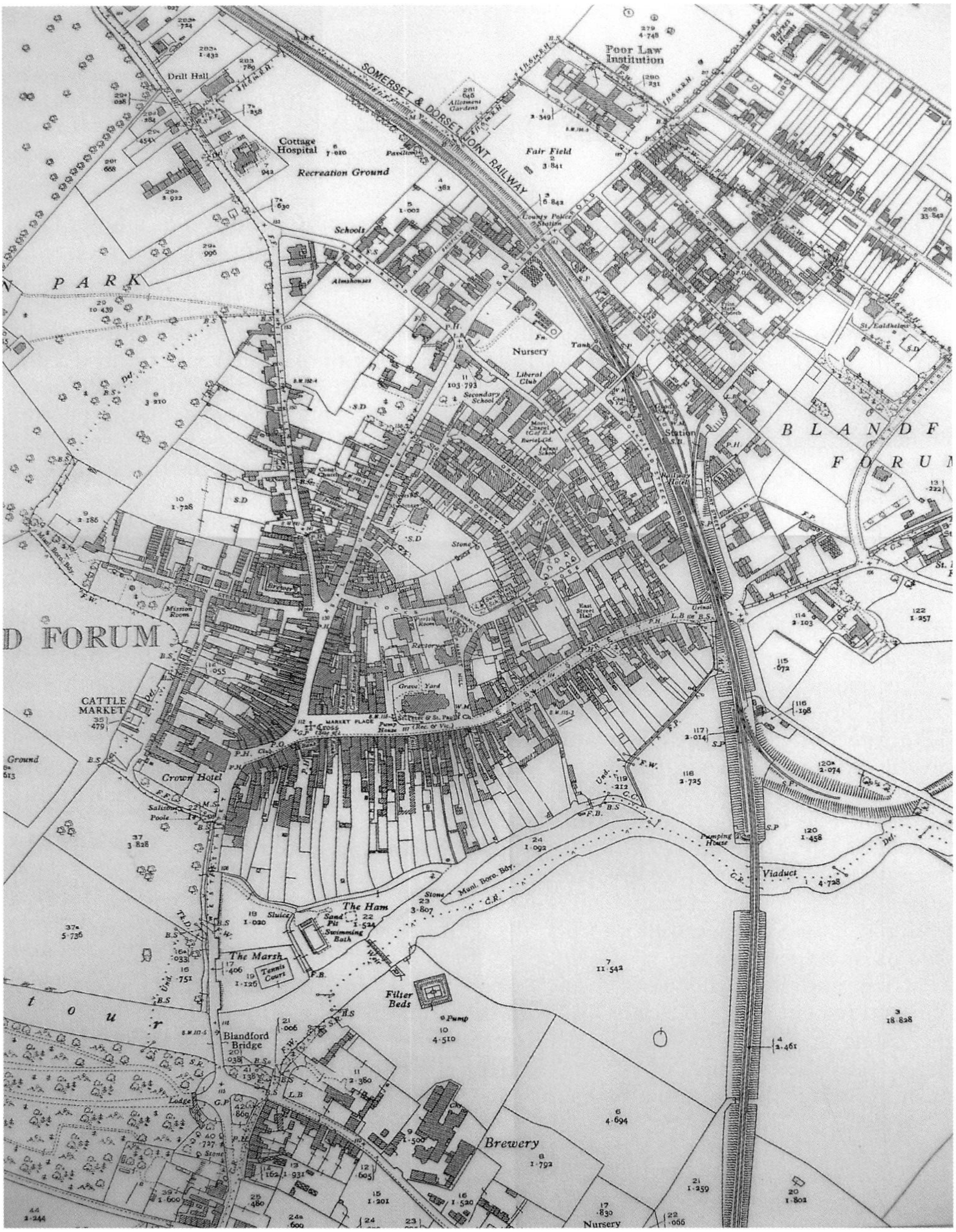

Blandford Forum
Taken from Ordnance Survey 25inch, sheet XXIV.7, 1929

INTRODUCTION

MASS-OBSERVATION

Mass-Observation, the social research organization for which Phyllis Walther wrote, had been established in 1937. It was created to meet a need; and that need, in the eyes of its founders, was to overcome Britons' ignorance about themselves in their everyday lives. Mass-Observation – it is often referred to simply as M-O – aimed to lay the foundation for a social anthropology of contemporary Britain, and to contribute to a better understanding of the behaviour and beliefs of the majority of the nation's citizens, not just its elite. Mass-Observation, according to a sort of mission statement in 1937, 'shares the interest of most people in the actual, in what happens from day to day'.[1] Its goal was to help bring about a 'science of ourselves', rooted in closely observed facts, for a proper social science, it was assumed, had to be based on evidence, methodically and laboriously collected. In order to pursue this science of society, M-O recruited hundreds of volunteer 'Observers'. These Observers were asked to collect facts, to describe, sometimes to count, to listen – indeed, even to eavesdrop – and perhaps to ask questions of members of the public. Their efforts at social recording were thought to be akin to those of an anthropologist working in the field. Mass-Observation, with hundreds of data-collectors working voluntarily in different parts of the country, was especially interested in casting light on matters of social life that had previously been largely ignored, such as jokes, superstitions, pub-going, betting on football pools, fears, habits of spending and saving, personal grooming, smoking, and 'Doing the Lambeth Walk' (a new and very popular dance).[2]

While M-O's volunteer Observers were normally expected to collect facts, an opinion developed among M-O's leaders that Observers could also function usefully as subjective cameras that captured their own experiences of living. This acceptance of the legitimacy of subjectivity in social observation was a major reason why diary-keeping came to be promoted as a promising vehicle of both social enquiry and self-observation. A diary was another way of recording, especially of things as they happened. The writer of a regular diary would be well placed, while memory was still fresh, to report on actions observed, conversations overheard, and other external events, not to mention the diarist's own immediate thoughts and feelings. From late August 1939, with another war on the horizon, M-O decided to encourage its volunteer Observers to write regular diaries – some people initially called their writing 'Crisis Diary', later 'War Diary' – in order to convey, as they thought fit and suited their temperament (no explicit directions were given), their own experiences of living in

[1] Charles Madge and Tom Harrisson, *Mass-Observation* (Letchworth, Hertfordshire: Frederick Muller, 1937), p. 30. In 2006 Mass-Observation dropped the hyphen from its name and became 'Mass Observation'. In this edition we have retained the pre-2006 usage.

[2] The range of M-O's interests is evident in a Penguin Special from 1939 (a half-year before the outbreak of war), *Britain, by Mass-Observation.*

wartime. A diary both encouraged and permitted an individual to see the world from his or her own angle of vision. By 1945 some 480 people had produced diaries for Mass-Observation, though many of these lasted for only a few months, and most were not particularly rich in detail.[3]

THE DIARIST

1. Phyllis Woodhouse in 1929

Phyllis Caroline Woodhouse was born on 2 May 1904, the third of four daughters (there were no sons) of Francis Decimus Woodhouse and Caroline Julia Woodhouse

[3] Nella Last, who lived in Barrow-in-Furness, was exceptional in producing a massive, detailed diary covering almost thirty years and probably amounting to at least ten million words of text. Selections from her writing have been published in two editions, both by Profile Books: *Nella Last's War: The Second World War Diaries of 'Housewife, 49'*, edited by Richard Broad and Suzie Fleming (2006; first published 1981), and *Nella Last's Peace: The Post-War Diaries of 'Housewife, 49'*, edited by Patricia and Robert Malcolmson (2008).

(née Witt).[4] Frank Woodhouse had trained as a doctor and was a member of the Royal College of Surgeons, but he was called back to Blandford St. Mary in 1916 to take over as Chairman and Managing Director of the family brewing firm, Hall and Woodhouse, which post he held until his death in 1952. He was a Governor of Blandford Grammar School, Chairman of the Cottage Hospital and Chairman of Blandford St. Mary Parish Council. The family had a long tradition of service in the army (Phyllis's Cousins Oliver and Harold died in action in 1940 and 1943 and five members of the Family died in the First World War).

2. Phyllis (on the left) with her sisters Isabel, Kathleen and Christine in 1910

[4] Her sisters were Isabel (born 1899) who married John Clerk Pyper and lived during the war in India and then Australia before moving to Tasmania; Kathleen (born 1902), who married Peter Joyce and farmed in Dorset; and Christine (born 1905) who married Henry Youle Huthwaite and lived in India during the war before returning to live at Grange-over-Sands, Lancs.

The family firm, Hall and Woodhouse, had started in 1777 at Ansty, near Milton Abbas, and moved to Blandford St. Mary in the 19th century. The firm looked after its workforce, setting up a company pension scheme in the late 1930s, unusual at the time, and making provision for the wives and children of employees called up for service during the Second World War. The firm is still owned and run by the Woodhouse family as a private company. The large, brick brewery buildings still dominate the small village and the brewery provides considerable employment in the area. Their Badger Ales are sold nationally through pubs, off-licenses and supermarkets, and they have approximately two hundred tenanted pubs in the south of England.

3. Hall and Woodhouse Dray outside the New Inn at Blandford St. Mary in about 1941

Blandford St. Mary, a small village and parish (population circa 280 in 1939) on the south-west bank of the river Stour, is virtually a suburb of the market town of Blandford Forum, which is reached by a stone bridge across the river. Blandford town grew up around the important river crossing which carries the main roads east-west from Salisbury to Dorchester and north-south from Shaftesbury to the sea at Poole. It is remarkable for the fine quality and uniformity of its Georgian architecture, the result of a complete rebuilding following a disastrous fire in 1731. This is particularly evident in the Market Square in the centre of the town, which is surrounded by fine brick houses with the Town Hall and church (also rebuilt after the fire) on its north side. Blandford was an ancient borough, with its own Mayor and council (Phyllis's cousin, Harold Woodhouse, was twice Mayor of Blandford before the war). It was the centre of Blandford Rural District Council, which administered local government to thirty-three surrounding parishes, the centre of the Blandford Poor Law Union, and had a County Court in which Quarter Sesssions and Petty Sessions were held. The population in 1939 was about 4,000. In 1862 the Somerset and Dorset Railway came to Blandford, which proceeded north from Bournemouth through Wimborne to

Blandford station on the east side of town, and then on to Sturminster Newton and Stalbridge in the north of the county, terminating at Bath in Somerset. Phyllis in her diary mentions travelling by train, but the line was a casualty of the post-war Beeching cuts and was closed in 1966.

4. Blandford Forum in 1941

Phyllis Woodhouse grew up in comfortable, indeed fairly affluent circumstances. Her family lived in Old Ford House, Blandford St. Mary, which was owned by and adjacent to the brewery. The house and its substantial gardens were on the edge of the River Stour, looking across to Blandford Forum. Phyllis was educated by governesses up to about the age of eleven; then she went to school at Talbot Heath School in Bournemouth, and afterwards read for a degree in botany at the University of London. (She had a life-long interest in plants and horticulture.)

Phyllis spent most of the 1930s outside Dorset. On 25 April 1930, a week before her 26th birthday, she married John Rodolphe Walther, whom she had met when they were both university students. 'J.R.', as she calls him in her diary, was from Norfolk, had Swiss as well as British citizenship, and at the time of their marriage was a civil servant. For some time afterwards he worked in government service in Nigeria, and when he and his wife were later together in England, they lived mostly in London, for a while in Dulwich. In around 1933/4 they acquired property in WC1 where they – in fact, mainly Phyllis – ran a boarding house for medical students. It seems they started with one Georgian house and later acquired the house next door; their addresses were 4 & 5 Torrington Square,[5] a short distance north of the British Museum and while the square still exists as part of the campus of the University of London, these two houses

[5] Phyllis sometimes used paper with this letterhead for her diary.

5. Phyllis and John Walther on their wedding day at Blandford St. Mary

do not, for they were torn down in 1935.[6] Later, in 1936/37, the Walthers acquired three houses on Guildford Street numbered 90, 91, and 92, just east of Russell Square, which they again ran as a boarding house, mainly for medical students. Their first son,

[6] A Canadian graduate student, who took a room at 5 Torrington Square in November 1934, spoke well of her accommodation there and (implicitly) Mrs. Walther's management of the house. 'They serve meals here, and darned good meals they are, too. And the house is full of students mostly male and medical. And all very friendly and jolly and, for the most part, serious workers. So at last I feel absolutely contented with my house.' (Robert D. Denham, ed., *The Correspondence of Northrop Frye and Helen Kemp 1932–1939: Volume I, 1932–1935* [Toronto: University of Toronto Press, 1996], p. 369.)

John, was born on 22 January 1936. Her survival to write the diary was a tribute to advances in medical science, for in 1937 or 1938 she had surgery to remove a brain tumour – one of the first times that such a procedure was successfully carried out in Britain. It is thought that medical students who boarded with the Walthers urged her to seek treatment after observing her involuntary leg movements.

With the outbreak of war in 1939, J.R. remained in London in his government employment, while Phyllis and her young son left London for Dorset, where they lived with, or in a cottage near, her sister Kathleen at Delcombe, to the west of Blandford, where her husband, Peter Joyce, farmed. Phyllis, her sons understand, helped with the work of the farm. Sometime in 1940 or early 1941 Phyllis returned to live in her parents' home, Old Ford House in Blandford St. Mary where she had grown up. Like many people in 1939–1941, Phyllis's life and the life of her family had been seriously thrown out of kilter by the turmoil of war, but at least she had been able to relocate to an area that she knew well and where she had close ties.

We do not know why Phyllis Walther decided to write for M-O or why she decided to start her diary when she did, but we do know something of the circumstances of her life at the beginning of the war. She was 37 years old when she began her diary for Mass-Observation in May 1941. She began by writing down some brief details about herself:

> Wife. Mother of one boy. Self-evacuated to parents from London. Formerly ran boarding house for students in Bloomsbury. Child attends a small kindergarten while mother does part-time [work] in WVS office. Father managing director of brewing firm in village just outside country town.

Phyllis then proceeded with her diary, the first entry being 12 May 1941. It appears that she posted her compositions about once a fortnight to Mass-Observation's headquarters. They are now archived in the Library's Special Collections at the University of Sussex.[7]

THE DIARY

A diary is an especially subjective genre of writing. Diaries can be very personal, even confessional, but they can also be somewhat impersonal, observational, and fact-driven. There are remarkable variations in the character of diary-writing, which inevitably pose different sorts of challenges for those who edit a diary for publication. Some handwritten diaries are barely legible, or at least include many words that are hard to decipher; others, from the twentieth century, are accurately typed. Some diaries are spare and economical; others are so wordy that it would be out of the question to publish everything the diarist wrote, and thus selections must be made. A diary may be uninspired and unremarkable during some months, while in other months it is lively, informative, and engaging. Diaries that are inward-looking and introspective may require little in the way of annotation, while others may mention such a variety of people, places, organizations, and public events that commentary and

[7] Reference: Diary 5454 (2).

6. Phyllis with John in 1939

explanation are routinely required. Editors, then, must adapt to the distinctive texture of their sources.[8]

With the exception of three-and-a-half weeks from the end of August 1941, Phyllis Walther typed her diary; and while she wrote something on most days between 12 May 1941 and the end of July 1942, on some days she wrote nothing. Thus,

[8] *A Soldier in Bedfordshire 1941–1942: The Diary of Private Denis Argent*, edited by Patricia and Robert Malcolmson (Bedfordshire Historical Record Society, 2009), covers fewer months in 1941–42 than Phyllis's diary, but since the original diary has many more words than hers (Argent was a professional journalist), it was necessary to publish only selections from his writing, and to be more selective for some periods than for others. The need to make selections for our edition of *A Woman in Wartime London: The Diary of Kathleen Tipper 1941–1945* (London Record Society, 2006) resulted in part from the fact that the diarist wrote for much longer, and that not all of her writing could realistically be published. By contrast, *Wartime Norfolk: The Diary of Rachel Dhonau 1941–1942*, edited by Robert Malcolmson and Peter Searby (Norfolk Record Society, 2004), presents a complete transcription of her diary for eighteen months, but gives only a brief summary of her continuing diary for 1943–44, when she was no longer working outside the home and had a less varied life to report on. Another M-O diary is too short to justify a book on its own, but since the diarist also left private papers that could be linked to this M-O writing, a book was possible (*Love and War In London: A Woman's Diary 1939–1942*, by Olivia Cockett, edited by Robert Malcolmson [Stroud, Gloucerstershire: The History Press, 2008]).

whenever a day lacks an entry, commonly at a weekend, this is always because she did not write on that day. Nothing has been omitted from this edited volume. It presents a complete transcription of the entire original diary.

A number of editorial interventions have been needed. Phyllis was not a skilled typist, and the typewriters she used (or their ribbons) were sometimes not in good condition. Consequently, her typescript diary includes many errors and rough spots. Some of these are obvious: a typo, a missing letter or other misspelling, a missing word (usually a small one, such as 'the', 'a', 'to', 'is', 'be', and the like). In all such instances we have silently corrected her text. In other cases, where her meaning is unclear or probably incomplete without an additional word or two, we have supplied an appropriate word or words within square brackets. Diarists – and perhaps especially those writing in wartime – commonly wrote in some haste and had little time or inclination to edit and polish their own writing; they did not expect to be published.

The other main changes are the following. (1) Like many diarists, Phyllis's use of punctuation was casual and not always consistent. In fact, she uses little punctuation beyond the full stop. We have frequently added punctuation in order to make her meaning clear. (2) She often wrote in short paragraphs. We have generally combined these paragraphs in order to produce longer diary entries, usually of a single paragraph. (3) We have standardized her usage of capitals and numerals, and have written in full the various names of places and organizations that she presents in a shortened form or as acronyms, either in the text or in the Glossary. Occasionally, when we do not know for sure what place she is referring to, we have written 'B_____', 'P_____', and the like. (4) The diary entries give only the day of the month, not the day of the week, which we have added.

Personal names – or rather, the lack of them – have presented a particular challenge. Almost all the people mentioned in the diary are named only by letter – thus 'J.' (her son), 'Mr. H.', 'R.', 'Mrs. S.', etc. We have handled this practice of partial anonymity in the following manner. First, when we do not know the individual's name, or can only make a guess, we have retained Phyllis's convention of identifying people by letters only. Second, we have replaced the letters with a full name when one of two things has happened. (1) Sometimes she has given an individual's proper name once or twice in the diary, almost certainly inadvertently, and thus we can fill in the blanks when that person is mentioned on other occasions by letter only. Thus it is almost always clear that the 'J.' she mentions is her son John, 'K.' is her sister Kathleen and "Mrs. S" is Mrs. Stuart. We have preserved her usage of 'J.R.' for her husband, who in fact makes only intermittent appearances. (2) Phyllis's sons, John and Julian Walther, have very helpfully advised us on other names, with the result that numerous people in the diary are now fully identified who, without their assistance, we would not have been able give names to. (A particular difficulty has been identifying people whose names begin with the letter 'R.', since there are at least four of them in the diary, plus two children.)

Finally, Phyllis wrote not only a diary for Mass-Observation, she also responded to its monthly 'Directives'. These were questionnaires, some of them fairly open-ended, about a wide variety of topics, and an Observer's replies to these questionnaires are known as 'Directive Responses' (DRs). Almost none of the Directive Responses for 1941 has survived in the M-O Archive at the University of Sussex. However, those for 1942 have, and some of Phyllis's DRs have been quoted at appropriate points in the second half of the diary. Whenever this is done, they are clearly distinguished from her diary entries. Two excerpts from DRs have been reproduced as Appendix C.

OTHER SOURCES

While the varied sources that shed light on Phyllis's diary are identified in footnotes below at appropriate points, two general observations are worth reporting. First, there were two main newspapers that circulated in the Blandford region. The *Western Gazette* was published in several editions; the edition that we have cited and quoted from for 1941–42 is that for North Dorset, which is held in the British Library's Newspaper Library in Colindale. The other newspaper was the *Dorset County Chronicle*, which is available on microfilm at Dorset History Centre, in Dorchester, Dorset.

It is unfortunate that, to the best of our knowledge, no photographs of Phyllis or her family from the early 1940s survive. Phyllis did once have a family photo album, and it probably included pictures from these years. Sadly, however, the album was stolen some years ago from her home in Swanage.

Finally, Appendicies A and B reproduce in full the accounts of wartime Blandford and of Bryanston, which adjoins Blandford to the west. These evocative portrayals of life on the home front are found in the splendid and unusual volume, 'Dorset Federation of Women's Institutes, War Record Book 1939–45', which is held in the Dorset History Centre.[9]

Most of the institutions mentioned by Phyllis and some of the distinctive practices of wartime are described and explained in the Glossary.

NOTE ON CURRENCY AND MEASUREMENTS

Throughout the period of the diary, the currency was pounds sterling. The main unit was the pound (£). There were twenty shillings in a pound, and twelve pence in a shilling. The sum of, say, two pounds, fourteen shillings, and eight pence was written as £2 14s 8d. The smallest denominations were a halfpence and a farthing (a quarter of a penny). Coins in common circulation were the half-crown (2s 6d), the florin (2s), the shilling coin, the sixpenny piece (6d), the threepenny bit (3d), the penny, the halfpenny and the farthing. Phyllis sometime expresses higher prices in shillings, e.g. 24s or 30s; these were £1 4s and £1 10s respectively. Occasionally items were priced in guineas, a relic of earlier times; a guinea was 21s or £1 1s. The modern decimal equivalent of one shilling is 5 new pence, so ten shillings would be 50 new pence.

Weights were in pounds and ounces. Sixteen ounces (oz) made up one pound (lb). The metric equivalent of one pound (lb) is approximately 454 g. When describing the collection of rosehips, Phyllis mentions the target being 28 lb, which would be two stone (14 lbs to one stone). There were eight stone to a hundredweight (cwt) and twenty hundredweight to a ton.

Liquid was measured in pints (for things like milk) or gallons (for petrol). Eight pints made up one gallon. The metric equivalent of one pint is approximately 568 ml. Phyllis mentions fruit being measured in bushels. This was an obsolete dry measurement, the equivalent of 64 pints.

---

[9] W.19/1.

Lengths were in yards, feet and inches. There were twelve inches to a foot and three feet to a yard. The metric equivalent of a foot is approximately 30 cm. Distances were (and still are) in miles of 1,760 yards. Items like eggs were usually sold in dozens (twelve) or half-dozens. Game such as pheasant were (and are) sold in braces of two.

ACKNOWLEDGEMENTS

We are especially appreciative of the assistance we were given by Phyllis's sons, John and Julian Walther, who provided much factual information, spent a day showing us around the Blandford region, and consistently gave enthusiastic support to this project. John and Julian also answered innumerable queries and gave us valuable insights into their Mother's family. Julian in particular went to great trouble to find family photographs and to help decipher the handwritten passages of his Mother's diary. Myles Huthwaite, grandson of Phyllis Walther's sister Christine, kindly supplied family photographs to fill in the gaps left by the theft of Phyllis's own albums.

Ann Smith, Hon. General Secretary of the Dorset Record Society, has played an important and highly constructive role in the production of this volume. She was active in locating and selecting suitable illustrations, composing several paragraphs in the Introduction and a number of footnotes that relate to County history, and raising various questions about the text that prompted us to make improvements and corrections. As a result of her contributions, this volume is significantly better than it would have been. We are also grateful to Matthew McMurray, the Archivist at the WRVS Archive and Heritage Collection at Steventon, Abingdon, Oxfordshire, for advising us on these sources, helping us to make good use of them, and ensuring that our visit to his Archive was productive. Frank Pike, former employee at Hall and Woodhouse, gave us a copy of his book on the Brewery during the war years and advised on other matters; and Malcolm and Angela Bentley, the present owners of Old Ford House, kindly gave us a tour of their house. The excellent staff at the Mass Observation Archive was, as usual, admirably efficient and helpful; Karen Watson's assistance has been especially noteworthy. Sue DeMille at Haynes Digital Services in Cobourg, Ontario provided us with technical support.

Patricia and Robert Malcolmson
May 2009

* * * * * *

Dorset Record Society would like to thank the Council of Management of the Marc Fitch Fund for grant aid. Dorset Record Society would also like to thank the Trustees of the Mansel-Pleydell and Cecil Trust for grant aid. These grants have made the publication of this book possible.

Dorset Record Society would like to thank Blandford Museum for permission to use photographs, and particularly Michael and Pamela le Bas, for their help and enthusiasm in finding relevant images. We would also like to thank the Dorset Natural History and Archaeological Society and Dorset County Museum in Dorchester for permission to use photographs, particularly Val Dicker for sharing her great knowledge of the Museum's photographic collection and locating relevant images. Suzy Cox at the Museum located the balaclava and mittens that are used as an illustration. Rebecca Donnan, Principal Conservator and Matthew Knowles, Reprographics Officer at Dorset History Centre, took an active interest in the book and provided images for us. We are particularly grateful to Matthew for designing the jacket. The National Federation of Women's Institutes and the Dorset Federation of Women's Institutes kindly allowed us to use illustrations from the Dorset W.I. War Record Book. Richard Samways kindly looked up information in the Guildhall Library for us and Dr. J.H. Bettey deciphered a word in the hand-written passage that defeated everyone else.

We would like to thank the following for allowing us to use their images:

Dorset County Museum, photographs 3, 4, 7, 10, 11, 12, 16, 30, 24, 25, 26, 27.

Blandford Museum, photographs 9, 13, 14, 15, 17, 18, 19, 21, 22, 23, 28, 32.

Julian Walther and Myles Huthwaite kindly supplied family photographs.

The delightful line drawings are taken from the Dorset W.I. War Record Book 1939–1945 (W. 19/1) with kind permission.

Map of Dorset on p. 6, copyright Dorset County Council.

Invasion notice on p. 132, Dorset History Centre, Local Studies Collection.

1941

Monday, May 12. Went up to the WVS Centre organiser's house as usual to do typing and odd jobs in the morning. It would be so much better for both of us if the aristocracy had a business training. Mrs. Stuart is the best kind of aristocrat no doubt – public-spirited, conscientious and very gracious – but we waste most of the morning in civilities.[1] Undid and sorted Red Cross parcels of needlework and did up parcels of comforts. We have still to dispose of a dump of flattened tins at Tarrant Hinton. If it is over four tons we can get a loading order from the Ministry of Supply. How can we tell how big the dump is? Wrote to the district surveyor[2] for help. Mrs. Stuart is also secretary of the hospital so wrote about arrangements for the cleansing station. Should have written about American Red Cross blankets dumped at Shaftesbury but discussed dog's health instead.[3] Fetched John from school. Great influx of new pupils from Army personnel. I can't afford the school but the village school was a mistake as he was the little rich boy there. I continue as we are with reduced fees and hope the education question will sort itself by the time he is eight.[4] Went to the Town Hall for blood transfusion. My first time. Very well organised and no waiting. All our village donors turned up and no one was upset. My arm felt a bit weak afterwards but otherwise no effect at all. Lying on stretchers drinking mugs of tea afterwards was the nicest part and the worst the injection, bringing back memories of hospitals.

Tuesday, May 13. A day off from the WVS on account of blood transfusion but no ill effects. Spent the morning and afternoon making frames for beehives. We shall need them full if we are not to feel the jam ration too badly. Tea at the Crown Hotel – a very showy menu for wartime.

Wednesday, May 14. To the WVS. There is to be a stiffening up with regard to the issue of evacuee clothing at last. I run the depot and as long as the village representative backs them, we supply applicants with what they want.[5] The Lord Mayor's Fund is kept for bombed out children but the American and second-hand

---

[1] Phyllis actually identified this woman as 'Mrs. A.', but this is clearly an error in typing. Mrs. Evelyn Margaret Stuart, daughter of Sir Edward H. St. Lawrence Clarke, Bt., was the WVS Centre organiser in Blandford. She lived at Letton Park, on the north-eastern outskirts of Blandford.

[2] The District Surveyor was responsible for drains, housing development, waste and other such things. He worked for the Rural District Council.

[3] The WVS was the sole agent for civilian aid sent to Britain by the American Red Cross.

[4] John was born on January 22, 1936. At this time he was attending St. Leonard's School, Blandford, which was in what is now the residential area of Fisher's Close.

[5] Clothing was collected to supply the needs of evacuees, families made homeless and others in distress and the storage of these clothes was often a challenge for WVS. As an official history put it, 'Practically no conventional space was available, so women up and down the land quickly found their own solutions. Small empty shops and houses, village halls, chapel galleries, outhouses and garages were "borrowed" depots.' (WVS, *Report on 25 Years Work 1938–1963*, p. 36.)

7. The Rains children, evacuated to Dorchester, date unknown

stocks have gone to anyone, often to the feckless and bad managers, because the children must not suffer when our own agricultural poor need them just as badly. Now mothers with their children must bring a chit from the relieving officer and unaccompanied children [a chit] from the school teacher. At the same time it is very difficult for a lot of women to adjust themselves to changed conditions and a Southampton woman transported to the country has no cheap or second-hand shops to go to and cannot pick up bargains as she sees them.[6] Wrote to Shaftesbury to see if they could take in an evacuated expectant mother in July. The usual maternity home here is closed for that month for holidays and spring cleaning. Took John to tea with Mrs. Killick whose small boy has started at the school. Her husband was working as an engineer building Blandford Camp[7] but has been moved back to London and is living as a paying guest in their own house. They had a furnished house for the first three months but now have moved into a large empty cottage and have lived there for nearly a year with the barest minimum of furniture, all borrowed from people's attics.[8] She seems perfectly happy. Her husband comes down alternate weekends and she works hard in the garden most of the time and is ardent Women's Institute and goes to two canteens.

Thursday, May 15. To the WVS. Undid parcels of village needlework for the Red Cross. Mostly very well made but most rural sewing machines need adjusting. They

---

[6] Many of the evacuees to the Blandford area were from Southampton.

[7] While most of the soldiers mentioned by Phyllis were probably based at this camp, some may have been working out of Bryanston (see the evidence in Appendix B).

[8] Mrs. Killick and her children lived in 'Milestone Cottage' in Lower Blandford St. Mary on the Bournemouth Road, about half a mile from Old Ford House.

cannot graft the toes of their socks and cannot learn or leave the stitches on a safety pin for us to do. The police rang up to know if we could provide a car and driver to take a Ministry of Information man on to Dorchester as his car had broken down. Rang up six people – all out. Found someone at last and directly we rang off the police rang up to say he had got a lift and gone. Went up the village[9] with WVS badges and forms. Lent Mrs. Killick our lawn-mower. Creosoted bee hives in reserve.

Friday, May 16. Attended meeting of Blandford Rest Centres. The relieving and billeting officer met the WVS and representatives from five denominational canteens and the organisers of the sleeping accommodation at the National Boys and Girls Schools, the Grammar School, and the casual ward. It all appears more efficient than we had feared but if these arrangements are to last for more than a day or two they will break down, as in every town. The Women's Institute are trying to get hold of a camp kitchen. The bakers can produce rolls in three-quarters of an hour and will bake stews. One butcher will boil stews and there are dumps of food at the casual ward and two shops. If the casual ward goes so does the Air Raid Precautions Control Room and the First Aid Post. We can sleep 300 easily, and more at a pinch, and there are always the churches, but blankets are very short. The relieving officer will distribute the food and blankets, soap and towels on the night. Dorchester is sending the cutlery and crockery according to a list sent to each canteen. The refugees will assemble at the Town Hall and be given coloured cards to indicate at which Centres they will sleep and eat, and marshals will be there to herd them. It may work if the victims are from another district but not if we are badly blitzed here and the personnel is all from the same part of the town, but Mrs. Stuart begged everyone to enrol as many helpers as possible. I think the canteens will find it very difficult to carry on if the essentials go.

Saturday, May 17. Was able to buy coconut oil shampoo just before the last bottle ran out. There has been none in Boots for months. Shoe repairs are very difficult. A week to put a pair of rubber tips on.

Sunday, May 18. Met Mrs. Fairclough at Sunday school. Her husband had got eight oranges from a canteen in Reading so her children were having a great treat, but the boy, who is a weekly boarder, said they had a half one each at school so the children are getting [lots]. Took John on the back of the bicycle for a picnic to Shillingstone Hill to see the bluebells in Bonsley. Tanks had been practising everywhere and every ride was blocked with little barriers but the bluebells were as lovely as ever.

Monday, May 19. Took John to a party and met the bank manager's sister, who had left Plymouth after nine raids.[10] They were lucky and still had water and a kitchen range, and being lazy after many late nights she missed the laundry and so saved her sheets when three laundries went. She has been working with a mobile canteen so might be some help here.

---

[9] When Phyllis spoke of 'the village', she meant Blandford St. Mary, where she was living.

[10] Plymouth had been heavily bombed on several nights in March and April. Details are provided in Gerald Wasley, *Blitz: An Account of Hitler's Aerial War over Plymouth in March 1941, and the Events that Followed* (Exeter, 1991).

Tuesday, May 20. Discussed personnel to help with the Borough food cards. In the end decided to ask an officer's wife who is a member and seems most efficient. The hours 10–5 will suit her as her husband does not come down from the Camp until evening. The district surveyor went to look at that tin dump. Only four hundredweight but he is going to find a few more round the district and collect them up.

Wednesday, May 21. Circularised WVS representatives in the villages regarding Red Cross Flag Day. Discussed starting a nursery school in the town as it seems needed. Advocated strongly that a trained personnel was essential for such a thing. A shower of rain at last. A cousin has come to stay for a rest cure. Her husband is the rector of a village and they have a family of evacuees. On paper their case is rosy but knowing them and how they can only just creep along we understand the need for the rest cure.

Thursday, May 22. Discussed a simpler method for controlling the issue of evacuee clothes. Got out a form that the applicant can fill in and bring with a chit from her representative, who can really find out all about her more quickly and easily than the relieving officer. On the form they must state the family income, any charge on it elsewhere, any special difficulties with regard to the present purchase of clothing, whether they have been bombed out or evacuated, whether clothes have been provided before and what clothes they need now. I think that this won't intimidate the ones who are in need and who won't go to the relieving officer and will keep the cadgers within bounds, and I hope as many children as possible get good American leather boots and shoes. Discussed conscientious objectors and the Army with Mrs. Stuart. It seems a great mistake to marry an old man.[11] She can't be more than 50 and yet it was a new idea that a conscientious objector[12] was or could be the result of the last war and not an evil slacker. She has no conception of a democratic army and was quite upset because some section had applied direct to the WVS for a wireless set. 'They are probably applying to everybody and selling them.' We referred the matter to the welfare officer. The thieving at the Camp and elsewhere is abnormal even for the licentious soldiery.

Friday, May 23. Went to my sister's farm at Delcombe and brought back three pints of their good milk. That will help us a bit. Everyone was much happier for the drop of rain.[13]

Saturday, May 24. The expectant mother can be taken in at Shaftesbury in July and went there for an interview but had had a letter from Wimborne to say that she could be accommodated there. Investigated the muddle and found that the new woman doctor had got that for her but as Shaftesbury is so nice our arrangement will stand.

---

[11] Her husband, Brigadier General Burleigh Francis Brownlow Stuart, was born in 1868. She was twenty years his junior (born 1888).

[12] A conscientious objector refused to fight on moral or religious grounds. 'Conchies' were treated with scorn by many people during the War, though government policy towards them was less harsh than it had been in the First World War.

[13] Phyllis's sister, Kathleen Joyce, is usually identified in the diary as 'K.' While we have expanded these references to 'Kathleen', it is possible that Phyllis herself would have called her by her nickname 'Kitcat'.

Heard from Plymouth that a friend there has been bombed out. Her father had a stroke and could not be moved out of the cellar for three nights and days and they had no gas or light or water. She has seen more of this war than anyone I know and her father had his practice filched away from [him] in the last war and now it has all gone again in the blitz.

Sunday, May 25. A lovely rain. Now we shan't starve. Went round the garden to see how the fruit is setting, though the bees have not had much chance to help. The frosts have done for most of the plums and peaches, but there will be currants and gooseberries which big growers have lost. Pears will be about normal. My Mother is going to bottle all she can without sugar. She sees to all that part herself and cooks without sugar, thereby saving a half pound a week. Seven people in the house but one is an old nurse of 93 and she eats very little.[14] The [two] maids eat all their sugar and John most of his but we do not have porridge. Thank goodness the cook went. We had one when war broke out but when the soldiers were billeted we were put down for ten and they wanted the attics, so all three maids were moved down to a large double room but she [the cook] walked out at that. We have thanked our stars since. Mother does all the skilled work and the overseeing and a woman from the village helps; she stays to dinner and has the old nurse's meat ration and is very glad to do it as her husband, who used to have all his meals at work, now is off sick and it was the meat ration she found so difficult. My parents have dealt at the same shops for 40 years and never owed a penny so they are very well treated as compared with evacuees or soldiers' wives.

Monday, May 26. Spent the morning in the stable loft with my furniture. We packed in such haste when we brought it down [from London] that none of the packing cases were listed, but now I have done that and I can lay my hands on anything we need for the refugees to the village Rest Centre. Spent the afternoon getting collecting boxes ready for Red Cross Day.

Tuesday, May 27. Answered a letter from a soldier's wife, safely tucked away in a farm in Somerset with her two little girls, and wanting to come to Blandford, put her children in a nursery school by day and get a job. She complains her husband allows her nothing and I suppose her friends here have written her glowing accounts of life here. Told her to get into touch with her local Soldiers' and Sailors' Families Association[15] about her Army allowance and that our nearest nursery school was Shaftesbury and that as she had a nursery training they might give her a job. I know the Waifs and Strays who run these schools at the request of the Ministry of Health need more trained personnel. Shaftesbury is a great help to us as they have something like 1,000 evacuees and we can see how much use is made of different welfare schemes before we attempt them here.

Wednesday, May 28. Took John to the dentist at Wimborne. I have not been since I saw my brother-in-law, who has now gone back to medicine so I shall have a lot of

---

[14] This woman, Maria Seabrook, had been nursemaid to Phyllis's Mother. Seabrook (as she was known) appears to have been a family retainer.

[15] The full name was the Soldiers', Sailors' and Airmen's Families Association, as she later acknowledged (see Glossary).

8. Maria Seabrook, nursemaid to the Woodhouse family

visits to pay. John had two holes which is rather depressing considering I lived on calcium before he was born and we have been tooth conscious ever since. He suggests he has them out rather than attempt to stop them. Perhaps we can have the car one day. A group of recruits have come to learn bridge building over the river. John seems to extract as much pleasure from them as we did from the Royal Engineers who were camped in the field there during the last war but I found I missed the smell of tarred rope which hung there permanently. These boats seemed very easy to handle and the whole bridge as simple as it could be. They built it twice by day and once by night and then a new group came.

Thursday, May 29. A day off to shop in Bournemouth. I came back most depressed. Everything most expensive, no two sizes of anything and only one fitter so when she went to lunch you were stuck. I found it made a great difference going by bus. We were tired when we got there and there was no time to go from shop to shop. Gardened in the evening. It seems a waste of time to bother with the flowers. We are making do with what is there and raised no seeds in the greenhouse.

Friday, May 30. Mother found a little brown sugar when she turned out the store cupboard and put it out for John to have with his porridge. Enormous reaction from him – ate a huge breakfast. More cases at the WVS. Mrs. Thorpe wants bedding as she lost hers on the railway, traipsing about after her soldier husband, and has never had a reply to a letter that she wrote to them. She is now having a third baby. The Motor Transport Service want to have a campaign for drivers. If they are married, they guarantee to give them leave at the same time as their husbands, and they won't have to go far from the district. A nice girl is going to demonstrate the cars in the marketplace. Went to D_______ to see my bees. The only conscientious objector I know well works there as an agricultural labourer. He is now getting married to a girl with a dairy inspector's job. No one has seen her but what we want to know is if she thinks it is all nonsense and she will change all that when they are married, or if she believes in it all.

Returned to find a pregnant woman on the doorstep needing an American layette.[16] She looked very ill and seemed to think that she was going to Dorchester Hospital to be confined but was in charge of no doctor here. Rang up her original doctor to find that she was a heart case and had been given strict orders to go to the doctor directly she got here. She has only a month to go and is completely vague. Really these women do worry one – they are so drear [*i.e., melancholic*] and so feckless. They must starve on their rations if they manage their housekeeping as badly as they manage their lives. I think that must be the key to the situation once they get in a muddle. They can't get enough food and then they get into this listless, helpless state. I wonder if communal feeding would be a success. One would [then] feel the children were having a chance.

Saturday, May 31. Ran Mrs. Thorpe to earth at last, hidden away round a corner in somebody's yard by the railway. Two children and another due in August and she has been told to prepare for a miscarriage so she must have sheets and pillow cases for the beds. The Army have lent her four blankets and she has two scratchy evacuee ones. We can give her American ones instead of the Army ones as she certainly deserves help. A most cheerful efficient person. All details for the confinement worked out. Her husband from the Camp gets leave at once and can be contacted through the Camp bus and the guard room up there and will look to the house and children and her neighbour will answer a tap on the wall and fetch the nurse she has booked. It was a treat to talk to her and find she had it all planned and all she wanted was bits and pieces. The children were nice too. Jeannie was left in the pram while I looked at the beds. Had the rations out and most of the sugar was spilt in the bottom of it. Her mother's comment was 'it only wants her to be wet now to finish it off'. We got it all out alright, however.

I have heard of a temporary job at the food office to do the ration books. I think I shall apply. Mrs. Stuart will let me go, I know. She suggested it when there was some talk of my being the forewoman in the brewery and now I have found out the key to her outlook I shan't feel I have left a job undone even if it leads to something permanent. I thought that if I could find out if she married the old General because her own young man was killed in the last war, then I should know whether she had made the best of a bad job or whether she wanted to be safe, and she has told me enough to know that she was engaged to him at the beginning of the war and married him before

[16] A set of garments for a new-born baby, usually comprising nightgowns, matinee coats, bootees, hat and a shawl.

she had time to do more than the beginning of Voluntary Aid Detachment [nursing] work – and that when her brother had just been killed and her father was going out and wanted her to be safely married. So her outlook is that of her father's generation and the Army at that [time], and with her brother dead she has had no one to open her mind at all. It isn't really a representative outlook for her class. The job I really would like would be interviewing for the evacuation officer but I am afraid that would be voluntary. It would be the nicest part of what I do now without any waste of time.

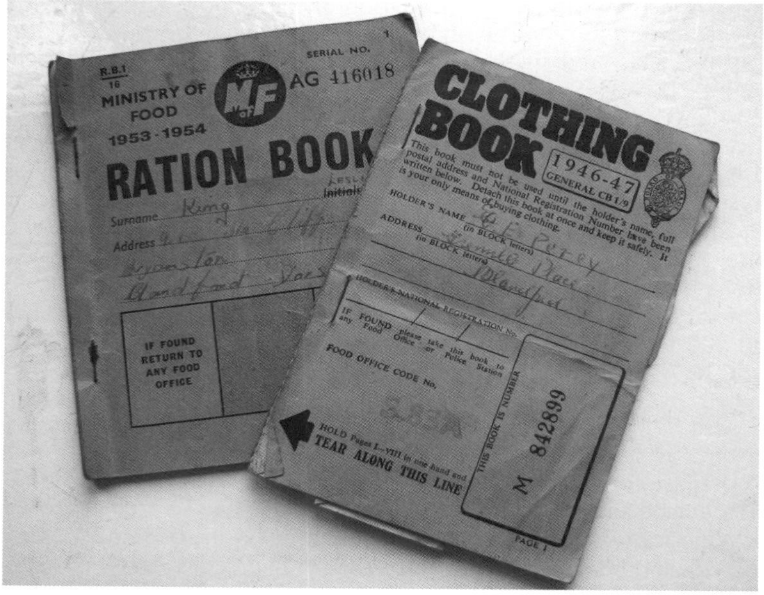

9. Ration book and clothing coupon book, issued in Blandford after the war

Sunday, June 1. We all feel we can manage with the number of coupons allotted. I find I used 153 last year for myself and 45 for John but most of that was buying forward and John has a lot of his cousins' clothes to inherit. Mother and Father both ordered two suits apiece when war broke out, having been done last time. Retired to bed with flu.

Monday, June 2. So glad my temperature remains below 102° and can still take charge of things and John in particular if the invader comes. Whit Monday isn't much of a day to be in bed in these days of rations.

Tuesday, June 3. Still in bed.

Wednesday, June 4. While the family were presenting prizes at the Grammar School sports, Mrs. C. rang up to say my bees were swarming in her orchard. It would happen. Sent wild messages to the brewer's mate and with the gardener's help the swarm was coped with. Turns out to be a minute hunger swarm from my artificial swarm which I should have fed and visited.[17]

Thursday, June 5. Got up to dinner. Mother took John to have his teeth out. He was overcome at seeing me but had quite recovered before that. Very unhappy until after tea when he completely recovered his spirits and thought himself a hero.

Friday, June 6. Up and about normally and very busy. It is suggested we keep a goat if the milk ration is serious. We had two cows in the last war but it was easier in those days and the cowshed is now a garage. Mother made butter and Wensleydale cheese. Rang up Mrs. Stuart. Things have not been too busy. She had been to see Mrs. Thorpe herself and Lady Stavordale of the WVS had been to lunch with her and had told her to buy her new sheets from a special fund, so that's grand.[18] I can give some cot bedding and everything is lovely. There has been a to-do over the clothing with the Board of Trade. The WVS was told to call a meeting at which their representative would be present and he never turned up and moreover was addressing a meeting somewhere else at the time and had never been told about it. Headquarters said there were WVS meetings ringing up from all over England to know where the said representatives were. When the man did appear at the Chamber of Commerce meeting, he was an accountant and had never addressed a meeting in his life and could not answer a question.

Saturday, June 7. Went to the food office and signed on for the job. Hard hours – 9 till 5 with three-quarters of an hour for lunch – and I know he slave drives, but the pay is 53s 6d [per week]. It seems very good to me. I was ready to clinch at 35s, which is what clerks in the brewery start with. I hope it leads to permanency but I doubt it. The night watchman [at the Brewery] has just been in to fetch the revolver from the office drawer. I enquired after his allotment and also a large stretch of barren ground up there which was offered to the WVS free if we could work it. According to this man, the Town Council has spent a lot of money having the allotments dug and then has not let them but a farmer has taken eight plots and ploughed them by tractor and will plant them presently – roots, I suppose. He thinks more soldiers should have been allowed to have them rather than let them get knee high in weeds. Thieving is very bad and difficult to check. An Auxiliary Fire Service man lost 30 broccoli when he had a run of fires and had to go to Bristol as well. A woman was caught red-handed with three but he had to let her go as she had five children.

Monday, June 9. Started work at the food office. A much nicer lot of people than last time. One ex-art teacher, 45, sister-in-law of the second in command, himself an artist; a sergeant instructor's wife, local; an officer's wife, South African born, 25; a boy of 17

---

[17] 'As a general rule,' according to one authority on bees, 'a swarm will settle within reasonable distance of the parent stock; but if it has to be followed over neighbouring property, care should be taken not to trespass without permission being asked. The old idea that a bee-keeper may follow wherever his bees lead him, is one that has no legal sanction. He should first ask permission, but if this is unreasonably withheld, he has probably good ground for action against the churlish neighbour if the swarm suffer by his inability to attend to it.' (Tickner Edwards, *Bee-Keeping for All* [4th edn,; London, 1934], p. 85.)

[18] Helen Elizabeth, Lady Stavordale, was the County Organizer for the WVS in Dorset.

who has failed his school certificate and been allowed to leave and wait until he can go into the Air Force – his father is a novelist and they are Roman Catholics. Everyone was well into the swing of the work, which is terribly mechanical, and conversation went on the whole time, led by the boy, Peter, and Mrs. W., the officer's wife. During the day we covered the following subjects: the cinema; our prospects in the war; current air raid damage; the Roman Catholic church; what is wrong with the church; life after death; ghosts; poltergeists; the exorcising of evil spirits; the Irish; the Home Guard. No one gave utterance to any rare or interesting opinions and Mrs. C., the sergeant's wife, was obviously not used to 'higher' thought and invariably brought the tone down to her personal feelings on any subject or her friends' opinions. The food officer's secretary tells me that they are going to amalgamate this Rural District office with the town and that will release three men of military age but the second in command is making himself indispensable so that he will not have to go. If he goes there will be jobs going for older women like me but if he stays he wants to run the office with junior clerks. He is a funny person and looks like a conscientious objector. He seems very unhappy and unsure of himself for a man of 34. His wife is nearly ten years older. Perhaps he minds being an illegitimate child.

Took some cot bedding up to Mrs. Thorpe after supper. The children were both out of the way in bed and she had sent her husband out to the pictures because he had such a long face and she had got on and scrubbed down the stairs. They have begun to cultivate the garden now that the billeting officer has taken over the house.[19]

Tuesday, June 10. To the office again. Peter was called away to superintend the storing of a load of sugar in a disused brewery. The tackle was not very efficient and one of the sacks broke open and ten pounds of sugar was broadcast in the street. The neighbours ran out and gathered it up in cups and basins. Discussions continued but not very deeply. I am surprised how conservative they are. No one expects a revolution. They are not very interested in the war except as a topic of conversation and only want it to stop so that they can get on with their lives.

Wednesday, June 11. At the office. Mrs. W's husband has been moved to Manchester. I should like to talk to her again after she has been in the industrial North. She says she does not want to go back to South Africa to live because, although the place is beautiful, the people are not so nice and Johannesburg is full of Jews. Both she and Peter find people in wartime so friendly although they know hardly any residents. But speaking as a resident, it is hard for us. We started off very well but no sooner have you got to know the Army wives than they are moved away and it is so difficult to ask them to meals or even drinks when food is a problem and time more so.

---

[19] 'The question whether Blandford Rural District Council should exercise compulsory powers in regard to the billeting of evacuees was again discussed at Thursday's meeting. The Chief Billeting Officer (Mr. B.A.S. Hicks) had informed the Emergency Committee that whilst the reception of evacuees had proceeded satisfactorily and all official demands on this area had so far been met, there was a very large number of householders who still did not realise the seriousness of the position, and it was to them he now appealed. So far the scheme had been worked on a voluntary basis, but unless he received a much larger number of offers in the near future a measure which must prove distasteful to all concerned would have to be adopted.' (*Western Gazette*, Friday, 13 June 1941, p. 3.)

Thursday, June 12. Mrs. C. and Mrs. W. discussed registering.[20] Mrs. W. very unwilling to sign up for the duration as she wants to follow her husband round while he is in England. She hopes to get a temporary job in Manchester or help with the harvest up there. Mrs. C. was an Auxiliary Territorial and is supposed to be going back but their husbands are against their doing anything.

Trouble at John's school. There are two adopted children, five and four, whose foster mother, an industrial psychologist, has sent [them] there as boarders. She has told the boy the facts of life and he finds that when he comments on them in front of the maid or the rather foolish house mistress he gets all the attention he wants so continues to comment on them and is then smacked. His form mistress tries to make up for his lack of love and petting by giving him special attention but his mind is in such a state he cannot concentrate or get on with his lessons at all. She wants to talk to the mother about them but feels it would be disloyal to the school as he ought to cease to be a boarder and go where he has a home life and a guardian with the same kind of outlook as the mother. I have met her – a typical university woman of 45 and far too sensible on the face of things to have sent the children to so unsuitable a school.

Friday, June 13. I am beginning to get my second wind and get home feeling not quite so dead to the world. A nice soldier's wife came for some clothes. She had had one baby since being bombed out at Waterloo and her husband brought her down here. We fixed the family up without much trouble. It seems surprising that they never know their size for anything – not always even for shoes.

Saturday, June 14. Pay day. After a week at that grind and purely mechanical work and no leisure I am all for the 35 hour week. I was offered a permanent job learning how to do permits to understudy Mr. W. but I don't know if I am justified in taking it. It means leaving John to others except for two hours in morning and one at night and in the holidays all his playfellows would be over 70,[21] and yet the money might make all the difference to him. John in bed with a temperature. Now I shall be able to try out the job business.

Sunday, June 15. My husband down for two nights. He thinks it is time I took a bigger place in the war effort and would like me to take the job or something like it. Suggests that I go up and see the Labour Exchange and see if there are any more jobs like this. He is very incensed against the civil servants who cannot interpret the spirit of the Ministry of Labour orders and cause unnecessary friction with workers and others. He seems quite unshaken by the blitz and yet I can remember his being in a panic when we were on a mountain in a thunderstorm after he had seen and been in tropical storms.

Monday, June 16. Asked for the day off. Not well received or graciously given. Married women are not in favour. I think my chances of getting the job are now

---

[20] Women were required to register for national service according to the year in which they were born. During June 1941, women born in 1917 and 1918 had to register; women born between 1910 and 1916 were required to register from August to December 1941 (the younger ones first).

[21] She is referring to the other residents of Old Ford House, though Phyllis's Mother was in fact under 70.

remote. Six hours to make up. Played with bees – took a swarm and learnt how to make up sections and was stung but not too unsightly. It was peaceful at Delcombe and my sister's life is just exactly what it would have been without a war. Perhaps they are rather better off. But with a farm and three small children and only the wireless for news she has her own anxieties so much closer than any war and no time to think.[22]

Tuesday, June 17. J.R. went back.[23] He has fixed up some petrol so he will be able to come again soon. Spent a completely exhausted day at the office. My writing does not seem so legible. I must have done too much washing and mending at the weekend. Mrs. C's husband turned up and she asked for the afternoon off. Major C. is afraid we shan't get done at this rate but we don't waste any time. It is a funny office. No one is office trained except his secretary and she is an embittered woman as she was got down from London with a salary arranged which enabled her to keep up the payments on her house but when she was here he told her he wasn't allowed to pay so much, but she stayed as she wanted to be out of town. She was also supposed to be second in command but Mr. W. has got that job so she does the skilled work and keeps apart. Stayed on in the evening to get my hours made up. Major came up to see how much work we had done. We talked amicably but he didn't respond to my advances about the job or about my wanting to be with John if he was ill.

Wednesday, June 18. Everyone on each other's nerves in the main office. Discussed women in industry and agreed conscription of women was impossible unless they could be sure of leave when their husbands came home. John taken ill with colitis at school. Rang up the doctor. How I hate having to leave him to Miss Smith although she is so good to him but she plays with him all the time and lets him behave anyhow so that he is never left to his own devices.[24] A lot of regulations about evacuee clothes. All the American gift clothing must have coupons and we must be very careful of pilfering. If there is a blitz we may clothe the naked free of coupons, but to the minimum of decency.

Thursday, June 19. John better after the medicine and no bad pain. I shall never get my hours made up.

Friday, June 20. John much better and very naughty about staying in bed. Pay day. I said I had five hours to make up still and the Major said I could make them up on Monday as the books would not be finished by then.

Monday, June 23. Made up five hours at the food office and took the rest of the day off and had a picnic with John and the Killicks. The Women's Institute is having a meeting about the jam making. They are going to tackle gooseberries first of all, which is an easy crop to handle, and then they will see how all the different members can do

---

[22] Phyllis's sister and brother-in-law, Kathleen and Peter Joyce, had an isolated farm about a mile north of Milton Abbas.

[23] Her husband's given names were John Rodolphe. In the diary she routinely refers to him as 'J.R.', and we have retained this usage, partly to distinguish him from their son John.

[24] Miss Ada Smith, an evacuee from Dulwich in South London, lived in Old Ford House and often looked after young John. Her nickname was 'Mitch'.

their stuff. Mrs. Killick is doing the tying down. Mrs. C. at the office is thinking of getting a job at the National Provincial Bank, which is very short-handed, and then she won't have to leave home. The news of Russia's entry into the war did make some stir. No one thinks Russia has a chance but they are dirty dogs anyhow. A farmer near the Military Police headquarters has taken to putting his fiercest bull in with the cows to intimidate the soldiers and their girls from going through into the hay grass. It seems most effective and the hay will soon be cut if this weather lasts.

10. Haymaking at Blandford St. Mary, 1940

Tuesday, June 24. Still another day's work to be done at the office. Five hundred children's [ration] books to be done. It seems very few for the whole of the rural area. There must be more than that in Blandford. Everywhere you go there seems to be a baby imminent. Mrs. C. told us how she got out of the Auxiliary Territorial Service. Five of the married ones got desperate so sent in their resignations and were commanded to an interview, at which they were told that they must present some plausible reason for leaving before they could be released, so they set to and made up various reasons and were then allowed to go, but one refused to tell a lie and she was also allowed to resign. She said you got progressively tougher day by day in the ATS until her mother said when she came home she was quite unbearable. She also told us what it was like here just before the war when the militia camp was being built under Government contract by Lindsay Parkinson. They were paid a percentage on their costs and the scandals as reported by men who went from the town to work up there were outstanding. The imported Irish labour were the toughest of the tough. They got digs for themselves at 15s a week, which was the sum allowed them towards their living expenses, and drank the rest of the money they earned. They would sign on in the morning and then come down to the town until it was time to sign off. She witnessed a murder when two who were fighting brained a man who intervened with a bottle and then kicked him on the ground. There was a tremendous lot of dishonesty about times and wages and when they were crossed there were cases of gangs shifting the huts they put up. She was working on the gypsies' cards during the morning and said they smelt most awful. A lot of them have to put crosses instead of their names but few have outlandish names except perhaps Britannia.

Our housemaid had to register today. She said she would like to make munitions and they suggested the cheese factory to her. She went down to see them in the afternoon but when she said she wanted to give a month's notice she was told the vacancy was the following week and she had better go back to the Exchange. She is due for her holiday and the other girl still has a week owing. The interviewer is trying to send them all into the ATS but the girls up at the Camp have a bad name in the town so that it isn't popular.

11. ATS at Blandford Camp, 1940

Wednesday, June 25. Mrs. C. and Mrs. W. have now decided that the Services are the best form of war work when you are married, as you are sure of getting leave and you can always get out and you do have congenial companions. The ration books hang on and tomorrow we are to come voluntarily but I shall be making up off time.

Thursday, June 26. Ration books finished at last. A few queries came in and we were very harassed in case they were ours. No pay until tomorrow and then only half a week, but having time to make up, it suited me. Went out in the middle of the morning to buy some tacks to put up new canvas on the garden chairs. They were amazingly difficult to get. In the afternoon I got John a pair of cotton knickers and was allowed them with coupons as they were within the specified number of inches round. This seems odd as he is five and overgrown. Had another paddling picnic by the river. Wonderful haymaking weather.

The agricultural workers scheme, by which we all volunteered to help with the harvest and stated what hours we could work and were issued with enrolment cards and armlets, seems to work wrongly here or else the farmers, being in a small way, do not want to pay the wages. None of us has been called upon and yet my Mother was told by one woman who had resigned that she had done some haymaking in the end because Mr. Moore had been at his wits' end to know how to get his hay in. I think it was a pity it had to be a paid scheme.[25]

Friday, June 27. Went to Dorchester with Mrs. Stuart to a WVS regional meeting about clothing. It seems a difficult question because so many mothers send down clothing from the towns for their unaccompanied children. In several cases they had sent for the coupons and then sent down very poor second-hand clothes and the foster mothers were afraid the clothes would last no time and when they need replacing the coupons would have all been used for other members of the family and second-hand clothes would be unattainable. We must be very careful of what we give out and part with nothing without coupons except in cases of blitz. Members of the WVS are to take part in the regular inspection of unaccompanied children's clothes so that new ones can be ordered in really good time. After the meeting I tried to shop. It seems impossible to obtain good children's clothes so that one would get something that would last or one could sell when outgrown.

Saturday, June 28. Stayed the weekend on the Delcombe farm. The crops look lovely and the hay almost in. The Women's Institute preserving centre in the village is having trouble over getting the equipment they ordered. The organisation is ready and the first fruit will be there and nothing else.

Sunday, June 29. My brother-in-law had a day out with the Home Guard. He now has a stripe and he is a guide, knowing the country so well. The mother's help has a daughter who has just volunteered for the Women's Auxiliary Air Force. She is 18 and her mother did her best to get her into nursing but it needed too much outlay.

Monday, June 30. To the WVS again and a lot of typing.[26] Notices to all the village representatives to tell them there would be a meeting on the 10th, that the billeting officer would like their help in the regular inspection of evacuees' clothing, and that the British and Allies Comforts and Victims War Fund would be grateful if they could produce 18 polo-neck sweaters in white for some naval officers engaged on a special job.

---

[25] Volunteers often helped with wartime harvests, though in this case it seems that payments were made for the labour provided. The records of Dorset's War Agricultural Executive Committee for 1941 include no evidence concerning the arrangements that Phyllis reported [Dorset History Centre, DCC/Acc. 6889].

[26] Mrs. Stuart gave the following report on WVS activities in May-June in Blandford and nearby. 'Some unaccompanied children arrived in the area. Arranged cars to meet and convey them to billets. Chief billeting officer for rural area has asked WVS representatives to undertake regular inspection of all unaccompanied children in the rural area in conjunction with the billeting officers. Expectant mothers and other evacuated persons and children conveyed to hospitals.' (WRVS Archive, Monthly Narrative Reports, Region 6, Dorset, Blandford.)

Tuesday, July 1. Flag Day for the County Comforts Fund.[27] They had the invasion scare in the middle of the last one and the word Dorset had to be cut off each flag. People were very generous. Went to see Mrs. Powell, who had a layette and a maternity frock from us. Her baby is due on the 12th so she was rather low in all this heat and her cottage was very messy. She seemed rather happy go lucky, wanting more things for the baby and making no attempt to get the things left from the other children from her own home in Bristol. She has let it now but is sending 3s rent up each week.

Wednesday, July 2. Heard from my sister [Isabel] in India, written just before she sailed for Australia. She has three girls too old to stay there. She said she was so thankful they had been able to get a boat and she had not to take them to a school in the hills. They are not inspected at all and are being terribly overcrowded with every possible epidemic. Nothing would be done until they had dysentery and a few deaths. They were trying to knit for the troops but as the wool shrunk in the hand with the heat and sweat you could not get a very good effect.

Thursday, July 3. Typed out notices for Hospital Pound Day. I can't imagine what they will get. Met the boarders from the school for a picnic. It was interesting to see the effect war food is having on greed in children. We have always been surprised that this generation has shown so little interest in food and put it down to their well balanced, varied diets but the boarders were really delighted when we produced a chocolate iced cake.

Friday, July 4. The district nurse called on Mrs. Stuart to collect her salary as she is the treasurer of the [District Nursing] Association. As Mrs. Stuart was busy in the kitchen with the cook we discussed our cases. She knew Mrs. Powell and did not think she was really entitled to any help as her husband was a sergeant and she had told her that her sister would send her all the things she needed in time. She also told me more about the maternity case with very bad heart who had not seen a doctor here. The woman doctor took charge of her and fixed her up for confinement. They were all very worried about her at the clinic but as the baby is so badly wanted and she has gone so far alright they are hoping for the best. The Stuarts are desperate about the coal situation. They used to burn thirty tons but cut that down by nine last year by having a small range instead of a large one and never having a fire until the afternoon. They have to have a fire night and day for the invalid aunt and her nurses. They could cut down a tree or two but he has only one arm and they have no labour. I could only suggest Calor gas and to buy small half grown trees called poles from a local estate as my Father does, which are very easy to saw up and burn well.

---

[27] It was reported this week that 'the provision of comforts for the troops relies to a very great extent on the cooperation of the general public and everyone this week and until next Monday has the opportunity of subscribing to the Dorset County Comforts Fund, when the Committee are holding Flag Days throughout Dorset. The money collected will be used towards the purchase of wool for providing the 177 working parties with wool at a reduced cost for knitting into comforts'. These 'knitted comforts' – scarves, pullovers, socks, and the like – were to be sent later to members of the Forces stationed in Dorset. (*Dorset County Chronicle*, 3 July 1941, p. 6.) Three months later plans were afoot for monthly house-to-house Red Cross collections to help send parcels to POWs (*Western Gazette*, 3 October 1941, p. 6).

Saturday, July 5. Went to Bournemouth for the day. No chance of getting to the beach but we had lunch on the front with barbwire and played with about a thousand other children in the Bourne. The gardens are left free with no restrictions except for a little bit with a fountain in it. The flower beds looked almost as gay as ever and the children had done no damage but what the stream will be like by the autumn I don't know. Anyway they all seemed just as happy as on the sand, only it seems a pity they did not make a big sand pit for them somewhere. We had tea in the pavilion ballroom, a useful meeting ground for the Canadian RAF and the evacuated banks' staffs.[28]

12. View of Bournemouth in 1946, showing barbed wire defences in the sea

Tuesday, July 8. Visited the Communal Feeding Centre at Hazelbury Bryan. It seems a great success without any fuss. They have a staff of a cook, washer-up and a voluntary overseer who helps with menus and the accounts. It was started by the County Council who sent round a circular by the school children to find out if it would be used by a large enough number and they have 60. There is talk of starting it in [Winterborne] Stickland as well.

Wednesday, July 9. Rang up various members of the WVS asking them to bring details of salvage schemes in their villages, if any, as there is to be a drive and we must discuss it at the meeting on Thursday. Most of the schemes have died out through lack of collection. Mrs. Stuart is to have a talk to the district salvage inspector before the meeting. Spent the wet afternoon making frocks out of the material I bought before

[28] Bournemouth was a major reception and training centre for the Royal Canadian Air Force (RCAF). The sea front was closed to all but the military and the beaches bristled with barbed wire, pill boxes, mines, and other defences.

rationing for overalls. I wish I had bought better stuff now and had given more thought to the pattern.

Thursday, July 10. The WVS village representatives meeting. Nearly everyone was there and the relieving or chief billeting officer. He told us that we must be prepared to care for as many as 100 refugees for as long as a week in the Rest Centres and the Government would guarantee the blankets and the food, which we must cook. Nothing would be distributed until the crisis arose. There was an immediate outcry from those who had had all their community halls taken over by the military, but on the whole we all had some idea of how we could manage, and he said that the military would be co-operative if they were still there. No one would back a regular inspection of unaccompanied children by an unauthorised person like a member of the WVS. They held that the children were already well inspected by the medical officer and where necessary by the health visitor afterwards and the school teacher, who also kept an eye on their clothes. If she needed help she had already applied to the WVS for help and anything more would be resented by the teacher and the foster parent. In most of the villages representatives and foster parents met often and knew each other well and inspection was quite unnecessary.

Mrs. Stuart described the Communal Feeding Centre and Mrs. W. (Stickland) said that the parents she had spoken to were much in favour of it as it would mean the rations could be saved for the fathers to take to the fields. Only one representative said the quality of the lunches brought to school had not fallen off. If cash and carry away meals were instituted they would meet with a big response in the agricultural districts. Spetisbury would have liked Communal Feeding as they have the greatest number of evacuees but they have no hall left.

Mrs. Stuart had had her talk to the sanitary inspector about salvage and reported to him that we were all willing to do our utmost for him but only if he would guarantee regular collection of the different kinds of salvage. Everyone reported trouble even about paper and it was urged that he should arrange with the Witchampton paper mills[29] that they should collect regularly from the whole area. Different villages had made various arrangements with them but they never kept any of them because the foreman and the manager never seemed to meet or pass on any information. They paid a good price and seemed more efficient than any other firm.

Friday, July 11. The housemaid came in from her holiday to say that she has had her marching orders for August 14th and is to go to Southampton for training in munitions. She has hopes of getting near Redbridge where her mother's evacuees come from, and then she will know someone and they have older children working from home. She is glad she has been away from home before, having been to a training school and afterwards to a place in London. The Women's Institute jam preserving centres are getting no gooseberries. A big grower said he was told by the Ministry of Food to sell his at 2d a pound which would not pay for the picking, but he sold them small as they get mildewed otherwise and he got a fair price, 10d. There is no fruit for sale in the shops except cherries at 3s. We are all making and bottling all we can. The Women's Institute have started a stall for their members' surplus. They only have it on

---

[29] The paper mill at Witchampton, near Wimborne, was established in the eighteenth century. It closed after the War.

Thursdays [market day] so that they will not interfere with the greengrocers whose wives are active members. It does very well and Mrs. T. told me she had already paid for her onion seed by selling the thinnings. She sells her fruit to a greengrocer and was getting 2s a pound for raspberries.[30]

Saturday, July 12. Had my cousin's evacuee, a boy of 8, to lunch and tea. He seems a nice quiet child but is supposed to be naughty at school. His father is an excise officer in Southampton. He takes his lunch to school and has a dinner when he gets in about 4. She can't make much of him although she has had a lot to do with children always and he seems very unsure of himself and not very happy.

Monday, July 14. Our little hunchback evacuee [Miss Smith] had an accident. She slipped off her chair when she was tending her tomato plants on the window sill and bumped her head and hurt her wrist. She was very shaken up but resisted all regular first aid and I left her sitting by the open nursery window with cushions round all the affected parts while I took John to school before the doctor came. When I got back she said she would like a cup of tea but would not have any glucose in it, and my Mother took care of this while I left and went to the WVS. There was nothing much to do there but shift furniture round to make an exhibition of the work we have done to impress the heads of the working parties and Lady Bruce-Gardner who is taking us into her region of the Central Hospital Supply Service and coming on Wednesday to make contact.[31] At lunchtime I found that the doctor had arrived about 12 and taken her up to the hospital to be X-rayed as he thought she had an impacted fracture. Mother and I thought what a farce all the first aid she had been doing was. After lunch

[30] See Appendix A.

[31] Lady Bruce-Gardner was the regional officer of the Central Hospital Supply Service.

I went up to give her room a good turn out so that it would be already when she came back, but when I came down again to fetch an overall I heard her talking to John, who was resting, and she had insisted on walking home and would not let them feed her or do anything but put on the plaster. My Father rang up later to ask matron when he should fetch her and she described her as an independent little Londoner and was touched by her refusal of state aid towards her hospital expenses because the Government needed the money so badly. She won't let her meals be sent up to her and refuses all help except letting the maid cut her slices of bread and me to empty a basin.

Tuesday, July 15. More preparations for the advent of Lady Bruce-Gardner. The room we have been using as a store was once the aunt's bed-sitting room but now she is bedridden she has half the double drawing-room and this room has the carpets from downstairs and a vast collection of furniture wedged in with dumps of various work belonging to the WVS, the American Red Cross and the Central Hospital Supply Service, not forgetting knitted garments from Ministry of Health materials. We were in the midst of making this look efficient and Mrs. Stuart saw a painted text on the wall. 'My old aunt painted that – it's a pity that the time for all that kind of thing has gone', and for a little while I felt the war was not being waged in vain.

Wednesday, July 16. Lady Bruce-Gardner arrived on time – most efficient but not a member of our older aristocracy – and Mrs. Stuart did not find her as congenial as Lady Wraxall.[32] The General could not find her in the right book and wanted to know if we had a *Kelly's Directory* of later date when we were discussing her afterwards. She said the work was very good and was nice to the heads of working parties who had come to welcome her and [she] wants all the garments marked in sizes, which is certainly necessary. She is also very keen on having a County depot of garments and dressings which can be drawn on in case of emergency, but as it has to be done from gifts and not from the materials sent down from headquarters and our income is very low compared with the first year of the war, it looks rather a tough proposition to me. We still hold a lot of our garments which we have been trying to give to various hospitals and at first we hoped we could make a generous gift of 50 pyjamas at once but she wants us to keep all that in hand as we are a sub-depot, holding quite a lot of other stocks sent when Bristol was badly bombed.[33] The new County depot is to be an extra special effort and this town being more central than Dorchester it might be near here. I think the remains of the Down House which was burnt out the other day would be most suitable and I could be the storekeeper.[34]

I had a letter from my sister-in-law, who had been left in Redhill with three small children while her husband has been sent to India. He was qualified as a lawyer just before the war and joined up and was some time in getting a commission. They stayed on in the house, paying no rent, and now she says that she has had no allowance since May but has sold a typewriter for £45, has one girl paying guest, and the Home Guard have requisitioned the dining room and store ammunition in the cellar, which was an

[32] Gertrude, daughter of Charles R. Shill, married in 1911 Sir Charles Bruce-Gardner, knight (Baronet 1945). Marceline, daughter of Mr. O. Cauro, married in 1921 Sir Charles Wraxall, 7th Baronet.

[33] Bristol was headquarters of the South Western region of the WVS.

[34] The Down House, south-west of Blandford, the residence of Sir William Smith-Marriott, was largely destroyed by a fire on 25 April 1941. The owner of the estate, an invalid, died shortly after.

elaborate gas-proof chamber at the beginning of the war. She says she has quite a social life as there is a club for officers' wives but she could do with a spot of married life.[35]

Thursday, July 17. Sent out the hospital's bills for Mrs. Stuart. Wrapped up two lots of WVS armlets for working parties. Began to mark all the unmarked garments. It is a good thing to have a thorough overhaul now and then; we shall feel safe from the moths until next year. Took some marking ink and camphor with me. Had a picnic with Mrs. Killick and the children. She is having to get her slippers made for a Women's Institute competition and in between whiles she makes jam and gardens with an occasional glance round the house. I am so glad she isn't going back to her house for the winter. Her husband was down at the weekend and put all the garden straight and had changed his mind about their return. Picked raspberries and redcurrants for jam; finished at 11.

Friday, July 18. More clearing up at the WVS. Visit to the dentist and more visits in store but I want to get done in case a job turns up. Picked raspberries in the pouring rain.

Saturday, July 19. There was a semi-public meeting to discuss Communal Feeding. Stickland could not have it in the end in spite of their representative's optimistic forecast. The County Council circular only brought in 17 demands for it and 30 is the minimum.

Sunday, July 20. A lovely day. The annual meeting of the Board of Directors of the firm and lunch here afterwards.[36] We haven't had a party for a very long time and everyone was so glad to meet each other. We had what seemed a grand spread – salmon (£2 worth), raspberry tart and custard, cheese and biscuits, champagne and sherry. The wives came during the meeting and gossiped in the garden. They were all in the Services in the last war and said it was a picnic [then] compared with this when they have large houses to run in remote places, and one a flat in London with all her friends away. The latter said the food situation was not nearly so grim. The last time they were down she took back a couple of rabbits and a brace of pigeons and half a dozen eggs. She has lived in Hampstead all her married life and gone to the same trades people and is very well served, having things slipped into her shopping basket. I also chatted to the chauffeur, who talked of queues, but his mind was very much more occupied with politics and the state of the Hampstead gardens than with food whereas the agricultural labourer is affected by nothing else. We concluded that the coal restrictions were brought in with no thought for people buried in the country. S. in response to requests ordered coke for her central heating – eight tons – and that is all she can have, but it won't do for any other heating and the coal merchant says he can't afford the labour or transport to fetch it and give her anything else. At lunch we discussed public schools. Malvern and Cheltenham, who had to move, have suffered

---

[35] Betty Walther, married to J.R.'s youngest brother Malcolm. J.R. was the oldest of 4 brothers. (Information from Julian Walther).

[36] This meeting is reported in Frank Pike, *Hall and Woodhouse Limited: The War Years 1939–1945* (privately printed, 2001), p. 53.

very badly as regards numbers and have closed as many as three houses whereas Sherborne and Marlborough are right up to strength.[37]

Monday, July 21. The secretary at the food office came in for her weekly bath but did not stay to supper as she had been followed twice running by a man she didn't like on her way home afterwards. It seemed a poor reason for missing a square meal in wartime, especially when she says it is difficult to make the rations run when you are alone.

Tuesday, July 22. Mrs. Stuart had to arrange transport from Shroton [Iwerne Courtney] for a bad boy evacuee to go to hostel. Apparently he stole everything he could lay hands on and his hostess said she would turn him out if he was not moved. In the middle of dealing with bees, a Mrs. McGarry arrived wanting clothes. She had come from West Hartlepool for the weekend to visit her husband on the Camp and had decided to stay on and had written to her mother asking her to send down her things and as they had not arrived she hoped we could fit her out with at least a new coat and some shoes. On investigation it turned out that she only wrote a week ago so I had to tell her we could not do anything for her yet but she could go and talk to the secretary of the Soldiers' and Sailors' Families Association. She looked the most feckless, unreliable type of person and had a small boy with her who was allowed to pick up and eat the hardest greenest cooking apple.

Wednesday, July 23. Mrs. Stuart had been to a County meeting for the District Nursing Association. There was a tremendous argument about giving the nurses a war bonus. Three percent is being found by the County and the local associations are to find another three percent of the nurses' salaries. It was approved by all, but some of the districts are so poor and have to find money for cars that they could not face it. At last the town open-air swimming bath has been cleaned out. It was built with a legacy and could not or was not made so that it can be cleaned out properly. The deep end is below the level of the river bed but with help of the fire brigade it was pumped out as far as possible and the bottom scrubbed with chloride of lime. The bath was never hygienic but now it is the only bath for a large number of troops and evacuees and 25 cases of chicken-pox were using it last term. It seems that steps have been taken just in time. We have been picking raspberries for jam and bottling all the evenings. The rain came just at the right time. Mrs. Killick had been able to get blackcurrants through the wife of a grower who is a member of her Women's Institute – and redcurrants too – but when she wanted more she couldn't have them. The greengrocer in the town kept some for her and also for our evacuee, but he had told her that too many people wanted them. I bought 2 pounds of lemons which John has had for lemonade but Miss Smith made lemon marmalade. I had a chat to the secretary of the Dorset Bee Association, who told me her war work was to take care of the bees of the men who had had to go. She promised to take me with her if she needed help and I should really learn something that way. The Government is to take over the inspection of bees. Two shillings nine pence a pound seems a good price for honey – for the producer at any rate.

Thursday, July 24. A letter from Lady Bruce-Gardner about getting materials coupon-free. I think we shall be able to help individual workers who have been making

[37] The number of students at Bryanston School had also declined by about a third to a low of 190 in early 1942. (M.C. Morgan, *Bryanston 1928–1978* [Blandford, 1978], pp. 73 and 76.)

13. Blandford's Open Air Swimming Bath, at the opening in 1924

up odd orders. They will have to register with us as home workers and order through us and theoretically we must check the garments made up against the materials ordered and send it [the order] off but in practice that would not be necessary as long as they wrote us a few letters to the file. I had a letter from the old lady I lived with in St. John's Wood, when I was a student. She wishes she could be dead and out of it all. They had a high explosive [bomb] in the little burial [ground] outside their house and the windows were out and the frames all twisted and the ceilings came down and nothing could be done for so long. Her old daily maid had had a baby and she had one who was no good and she was tired of trying to keep a home for her two daughters, an almoner[38] and a masseuse, both out most nights on warden and first aid posts. We wanted her to come down here but she won't leave them even for a little while – and she hates the country.

Friday, July 25. Mrs. Stuart has been asked to increase the clothing depot to keep the stocks dispersed. That means us but there would be plenty of room for bales but not for display unless we had the room shelved. Went up the town in the afternoon to fetch a pram which was presented to the WVS. When I got there we found it was broken underneath but after taking it from shop to shop a garage said they could solder it and it is a good pram so it is worth doing.

Saturday, July 26. Spent a morning on my furniture and bedding, getting it into shape for the peace. There is a terribly optimistic feeling about, as if the war were really going to end.[39]

---

[38] An almoner is a social worker in a hospital.

[39] This short-lived optimism was due to the German invasion of Russia. Since the Germans had turned their attention to the east, this reduced the threat of invasion and took the pressure off Britain.

Sunday, July 27. Mrs. Stuart very much occupied with her notes for the hospital meeting this afternoon. The authorities have just realised that it will be outside the island of defence[40] in case of invasion and have asked what we are going to do about it. Marked clothes that the WVS are giving to the gas cleansing station. They have been waiting so long in the garage to be delivered that I had to take them all out and hang them on the fences round the park. Received a lot more second-hand clothing for the depot. It would be so much pleasanter if people would do a little sorting before they send it. I loathe washing other people's dirty clothes, but mending isn't so bad because they could not make the time to do it. My sister's nurse, who has only been there three weeks, seems to be having a nervous breakdown.

Monday, July 28. Kathleen's nurse has gone mad. Her eldest (3) [Thomas] has come here and Mother has gone over to help. I shall have to housekeep. Only wrote letters at the WVS to the Personal Service League for patterns of wools and pyjama materials; to the education officer at Southampton for a voucher to purchase one of his evacuees shoes as her mother can't afford them though she has provided the rest of the clothes needed;[41] and to the Women's Land Army about a girl who came up in the last Junior Court and was sent to a remand home but is keen on farm work so Mrs. Stuart wanted to know if there was a suitable place in the district where she could do it and have some supervision.

Tuesday, July 29. Delivered the small boys at school. It is breaking up. Returned to the housekeeping. Our daily cook is most kind and helpful so it seems a picnic this time when she hasn't got flu. It is very good for me. I find I curb my appetite when I know things are short. Sent out circulars to all the representatives about cotton reels, which are in great need for the Royal [Corps of] Signals.[42] Went round to the village dressmakers to ask them to save theirs. Heard all about the nurse. Apparently she has had attacks something like this before but has always been at home and been given a powerful sleeping draught. It begins with sleeplessness. She had tried to have charge of all three children and my sister gave in and thought she would let her have her own way to start with but had taken full charge of the baby again before the final attack. As she became worse she seemed to cling to the method of doing things and became slower and slower until method was all that was left and they spent the whole night walking along the passage and back, first with one foot and then with the other, and going backwards down the stairs. The doctor gave her a sedative but of course had no idea what she had been given before and it had no effect at all. Her mother was rather

---

[40] The island of defence, or tank island, was the area of Blandford within the military defences. These comprised 'dragon's teeth' or concrete blocks, temporary road blocks and 'pill-boxes' or gun posts. Details of the Blandford's defences are presented in Major E.H.R. Schmidt, *The Defences of Blandford Forum: A short history of the Second World War Defences* (Blandford Forum Museum Trust, 1987), Dorset History Centre, Local Studies Collection BLA, D6:9, 355.58, '1939'.

[41] Earlier this year, after the bombing of Southampton had caused several hundred children to be evacuated to the Blandford area, Mrs. Stuart reported that 'American clothing and boots have been of great assistance to the children, many of whom are very rough and come from poor and large families who cannot provide much for them.' (WRVS Archive, Monthly Narrative Reports, Region 6, Dorset, Blandford, January 1941.)

[42] The cotton reels were probably required as insulators for field telephone installations (information kindly supplied by Col. Mike Butler and Tim Stankus of the Royal Signals Museum, Blandford Camp).

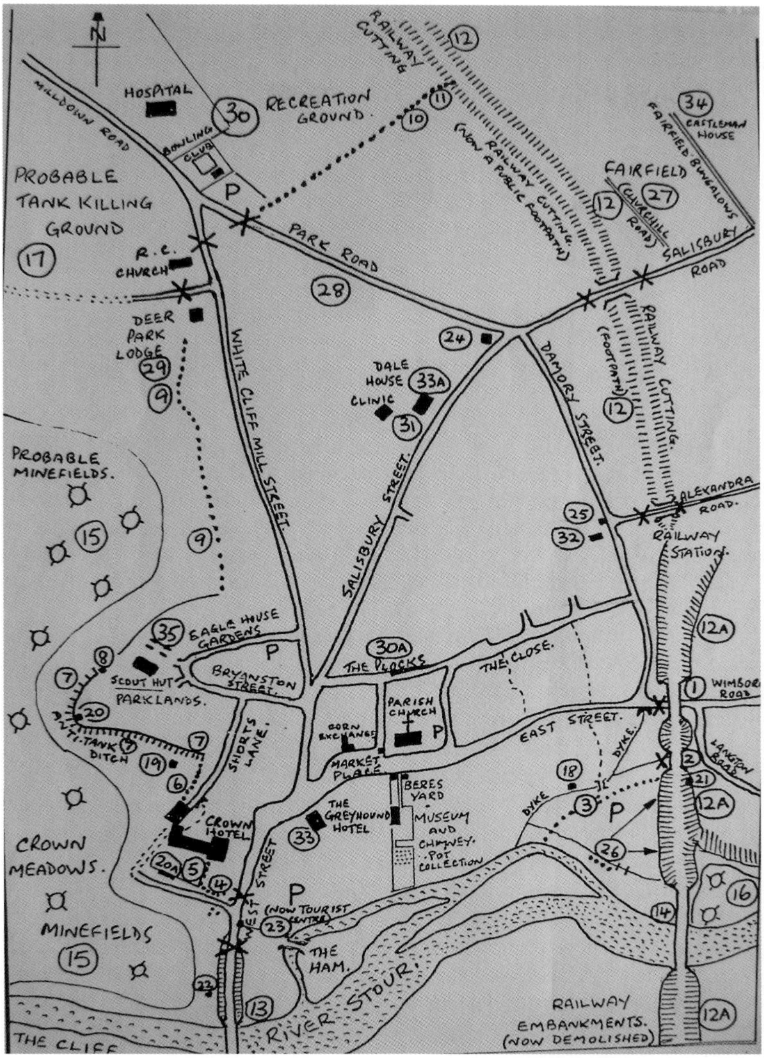

14. Map of the Island of Defence around Blandford

to blame for letting her come away without a doctor looking after her because she would never have got so bad if she had gone to him when she stopped sleeping.

Wednesday, July 30. Left the boys with their form teacher who has come for a few days. She says John will read by Christmas so I must give notice for him then because I don't want him to waste time in the next form with an ex-ballerina when he can go to the Grammar School. The Stuarts had the day off to see an aged relation who has broken her thigh so I had a quiet morning sizing socks and writing odd notes. Two evacuees turned up for clothes who had a lot once before. I was out, happily, because with all the new regulations it takes some time to sort them out. These are soldiers' wives and have over £2 a week each so they are not entitled to any more from us unless the [Public] Assistance Board recommends them but I don't think he will as the Army allowance is supposed to allow for clothing and they have no outgoings.

Thursday, July 31. Had a day off to go to Bournemouth with the children. The bus was packed but we got seats in the end. Visited the toyshop. Beales[43] was full of stuff and might have been pre-war but for the prices. We had lunch on the beach as there was a way made through the wire. It became crammed soon after but it was lovely to be there.[44] A fishing boat came in and sold fish to all comers, mostly mackerel and plaice. There was no shortage of customers. We had tea at Stewarts where the waitress stole a little extra milk for the children. I managed to buy a quarter [pound] of sucking sweets and a half pound slab of chocolate which the children suggested would do instead of cake.

Saturday, August 2. Cooked and housekept until lunch. Curried the last of the week's rabbits and managed some fish for the children. We can have our next week's biscuits on Saturday so I shan't have to try to make any. Took the children for a picnic by the river. We went too far and Thomas cried. I get so used to being with other mothers whose one idea is to get somewhere suitable quickly and sit down with one's knitting that it was quite difficult to adjust myself to finding a romantic spot.

Monday, August 4. Our poor evacuee had her arm out of plaster and is more unhappy than ever. She likes matron very much but longs for her old doctor in London and I am sure thinks it will never get right down here. The town was packed out with soldiers' wives last night.[45] The husbands do nothing about rooms for them in many cases and go from door to door last thing at night and no one will take them in if they can help it as they bring no food with them. We really need a hostel for them but it would be impossible to get the house with the military in every empty one. The police station was besieged in the end and a lot of the weekenders were housed in the casual ward under the supervision of the ARP people.

We had mail from Australia at last. They had no excitements on the way except a threatened tornado and were landed at Sydney and sent on to Melbourne by train at the Company's expense. The children are revived already and my sister is so glad she went. Everything is so expensive, especially clothes, and she is glad she bought all she could in India. Prams cost about £4 for the cheapest, so that is about the same as in this country.

My sister and her husband from the farm came in on their way back from a visit to his brother outside Oxford to fetch a load of furniture stored there by an aunt who was bombed out of Dulwich and, knowing she will never have a home again, is willing to let them have it to let a house furnished. They are always held up so giving soldiers lifts in the trailer, which holds a good many, and as soon as it is packed up they have to

---

[43] Beales was (and is) a large department store in Bournemouth.

[44] These special arrangements for daytime sea bathing, which took effect from July 12th, are noted in M.A Edgington, *Bournemouth and the Second World War* (Bournemouth, 1994), p. 48.

[45] This was a Bank Holiday weekend.

start stopping to let them get out. She has not got a nurse yet, but a temporary is coming on the 18th, so we shall have Thomas until then, which suits me very well as he can be a boon companion for John.

The girl from the food office came in for tea and a bath. Her chief is having sick leave for a month so perhaps he will be better after that. The food for the villages is to be distributed throughout the villages, which does seem more sensible. We are to have a dump in our attic, probably for here – 90 cubic feet are required. In case of invasion and no one allowed on the roads, they will be able to get to this house by the fields as all the houses are this side as there was originally a lower road.

Tuesday, August 5. SOS about Kathleen's joint. She went off yesterday and it was still in our fridge.[46] It is all my fault. Went to the inn yard where their village used to pick up parcels. The soldiers have all that now and the bus waits outside the Crown Hotel and has no office. The woman at the pub, which is one of the firm's [*i.e., owned by Hall and Woodhouse*] – and she used to get her milk from the farm – said she would send it across when the bus was there.[47]

Circularised the WVS representatives about the Assistance Board's mobile van which is to be ready to go to blitzed areas and assist the homeless. They are to have sleeping and cooking arrangements in a separate van which makes a base in a village outside the target area and want the WVS to take care of the [*word missing*] and find a place for them to have their meals and help in their preparation and service. The County Public Assistance man came over to see Mrs. Stuart and to settle a few slight differences which seem to exist between the Public Assistance man here and the warden of the Public Institution, which is also the First Aid Post and control room and has to sleep 60 people in the case of a raid. He told her that if the Public Assistance man was killed his job fell to her, so God help us all.

Walked to a village five miles out with a pram for a new evacuee baby. Happily it was a nice one and John had a ride out and walked back most nobly. The woman was so nice. This was her third and she had been in her billet with a farmer's widow for a year. They liked her so much. She had a big room upstairs which would take them all and her husband when he got a holiday and a ground floor sitting room where her friends could come in without disturbing anyone in the house. They want a cot for the baby when it gets a bit older because at present it is sleeping in a drawer.

Wednesday, August 6. The housemaid heard from her brother in Malta. They can't tell you any news and say you must depend on the wireless. He has written every mail but this is only the second letter she has had this year. I brought home some typing to do but I was to be the only one in the house to listen for the children. Lydia is having her last fling before she goes to Southampton to train for munitions and was off for a dance. The hall is terribly crowded. The soldiers generally get shoes to dance in and one had a pair which were two sizes too big. The Military Police used to try to send

---

[46] John Walther remembers a tall fridge in the scullery at Old Ford House. Domestic refrigerators did not become widely available in this country until the late 1950s, so they were fortunate to have this convenience.

[47] Three carriers ran motor omnibus services to Blandford from the Milton Abbas district: Milton Abbas Motors (Sprackling), House brothers of Hilton and Sidney Harmer of Milton Abbas. The latter is the only one who ran services to Blandford on Tuesdays so is likely to be the carrier mentioned here.

them in again to put on their boots if they went out between dances but that has been stopped now. She has heard of several people who are in Redbridge now so she isn't quite so apprehensive. Our daily cook says her son had his first flight. He was a chauffeur before the war, had never left his first job, and now he has passed all his exams and is making aircraft and they have to put their initials under every bolt they put in so that they know who is responsible for good and bad work. The boy who worked in the garden has finished his air gunner's training too and came home to show his stripes.

Thursday, August 7. Circularised the WVS representatives about Air Raid Distress Fund. Got the tins ready to send out. There are new rules for the issue of clothing. We now have an order from the Assistance Board at Weymouth to provide certain people with clothing to make up their clothes to a standard to which coupons can be applied fairly. A new maid has arrived instead of Lydia. She has been eight years with an old lady in Bournemouth and felt she could not face another winter fire-watching. My Mother has returned so my mind will be free from the food jigsaw puzzle. I was lucky because we have been able to have liver and kidneys this week. Kathleen's joint never caught the bus in the end. I retrieved it and sent it out by the car which fetched Mother home. It had gone high but I opened it out and poured boiling water on the livestock and then roasted it and it smelt quite normal in the end, and anyhow Peter likes his meat well hung so I expect it won't be wasted. Their nurse was certified as insane when she got home.

Friday, August 8. Mrs. Stuart told me they are going to start a British Restaurant in Blandford. It will be in the parish room and they have to make a few alterations first. It will seat 50 then and they will have two relays. The first will be for school children and the second for evacuees. They want an overseer to help with the accounts and menus and to see the people in and then a whole lot of helpers to take it in turns to serve. The cook and washer-up will be the only paid staff. Met a woman who has been helping in a nursery school in Devon. They were neither of them trained but both paid. It was held in the parish room and her work consisted of conducting the little ones through the church to get to the lavatory. They loved this and whenever possible bolted into the pulpit. She told us their favourite game was air-raids, which they instantly resorted to if left to themselves, but this the helpers discouraged, which goes to prove how wise the authorities are to advise a trained personnel because all the child psychologists seem agreed in advising the encouragement of such play so that the air raid becomes a friendly thing and the fear is played out. The Women's Institute has tied down 160 pounds of jam and is doing another 60 tomorrow. It is mostly rhubarb and redcurrant, and rhubarb and raspberry.

Saturday, August 9. Fitted out the first evacuee with clothes under the Assistance Board's recommendation. Her WVS representative thought she had told the tale and was no more deserving than many others. She was an old lady from the Docks and still looked the complete Londoner although she has been buried in the country since the autumn. I could only manage underclothes and had to take her to Frisby's[48] to choose a pair of shoes and have them put aside until the voucher and the coupons come. We

---

[48] Joseph Frisby Ltd. was a shoe-shop in the market place in Blandford.

had another meeting of the Board of Directors. No wives this time. Charles,[49] who is in Plymouth, said that the town surveyor went to the military and said quietly that he would like all the centre of town reduced to ten feet so that it would count as a cleared area. So the Royal Engineers were put on to deal with it and now it is all ready for a nice straightforward bit of town planning without anyone to interfere.

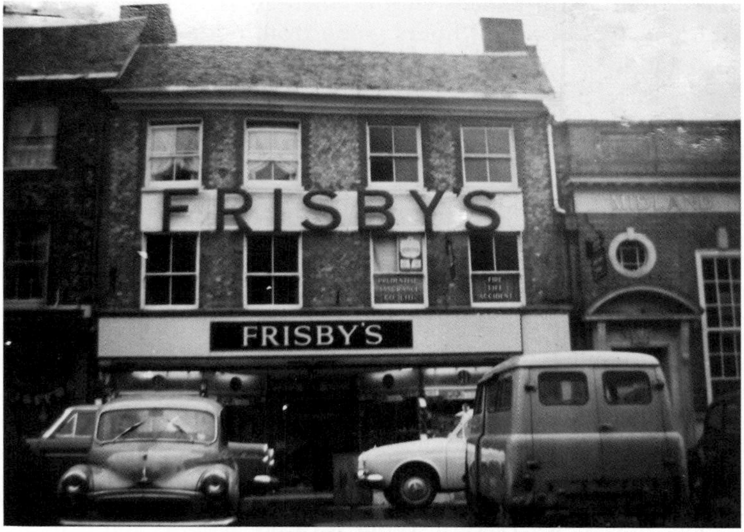

15. Frisby's shoe shop in Blandford Market Place, taken in the 1960s

Monday, August 11. Sent out circulars for yet another Flag Day. Air Raid Distress Fund this time. It seems a pity they could not have it in the winter when our sympathies will be more roused. We are to have a food dump in the attic, 6s worth for each person, and it is to be kept dark so that the village will not ease up on their own stores. If a household is too numerous to pay out for everyone, they are to be helped. This dump is for the local residents but the Public Assistance Board is also releasing food and blankets to be stored in the Rest Centres against an emergency when we are to expect refugees. A mother and two wild children came to tea. She is half Swiss and has been living with a sister-in-law at Basingstoke. She said things seemed much easier here as far as cakes, fruit and potatoes went and many groceries too. Her in-laws have been there for five years so they ought to be fairly well treated. The town is so full that the elder boy could not get into the school his cousins are at and goes to another where the hours are quite different, which makes the meals very difficult. They were the toughest children I have seen for sometime and were staying in a small house where they had no room and no toys and it was too wet for the garden. My nephew Thomas is to come to us next term and start at the nursery school. It will be very good for John but I see myself being very war weary by Christmas.

---

[49] See note to 2 June 1942.

Tuesday, August 12. A day at home with bees, blankets and children. Patched some pyjamas for the clothing depot. Two huge bales of clothing from America arrived.

Wednesday, August 13. The maid's sister who was discharged from the ATS came in. She is waiting to hear from her husband to know if he can get a room for her in a village 16 miles from Perth. She went up there once on the chance of getting accommodation and they spent 12 hours going from door to door. She thought the Scotch very odd and 'they treat you like a foreigner and like to know things a week in advance'.

Thursday, August 14. Another day at home spent gardening – replanting the bulbs. It has not been done since my elder sister was at home with time to waste. I must be about in the garden with the children. Took them up to the Milldown to the swings. It is a nice healthy place outside the town but there were hardly any children up there although it is holiday time.[50] They all come down to the river and the swimming bath whatever the weather is like. My parents went to a Governors' meeting at the Grammar School. They are going to build a dining room for the pupils and have communal feeding. A hundred [pupils] bring dinners daily and many of them have been having dry bread and 2d to buy a pastry. The headmaster got some bully-beef which he gave them to go with it. It will take a little while to get ready but the site is close to the school, which has appalling buildings now.

Friday, August 15. Mother went over to my sister's taking Thomas with her so John and I had a quiet day. It was very wet and we were indoors until the evening. My Father fetched them home and collected mushrooms on the way as well as calling at the maltings with the wages and delivering three parcels of flags and evacuee clothing to the WVS representative at Milton Abbas.

Monday, August 18. Thomas returned to his own home. My sister came in and met a temporary nurse and took them both back. She was our maternity nurse but has few maternity cases at present so has been with an old lady who had a marvellous operation on her broken thigh and can now walk again at the age of 80. I do not think the lack of proper cases is due to the war but to the fact that she is getting old and her patients and their friends are getting past child bearing. She told us that there was a shortage of tomatoes in London so I have sent some off to friends in NW. They ran out of petrol on the way home, happily just outside our gate, and we had a can. Thomas in flood of tears in case he should not get home.

Tuesday, August 19. Mr. B. has a rick on fire – £200 gone west so someone estimates. It was all his own fault because other people passing smelt it during the weekend and he passes it several times a day going from one farm to another. My Father was very angry, being a member of the Rural District Council, as it has to pay for the fire engine according to the new fire regulations. It seems rather wrong as Mr. B. is rich as well as

---

[50] The Milldown is a grassy and wooded area of 40 acres on the north-western edge of Blandford.

careless.[51] Went for a boating picnic in a leaking boat, which was great fun. The only other boat happened to contain a girl I had not met for years and she was only there for the afternoon from Bournemouth. She is a masseuse in Birmingham and having her first holiday for two years as in '39 she was recalled after two days and last year she could not move from Bournemouth as it was a strict defence area.

Wednesday, August 20. The voucher and coupons came from the Assistance Board for Mrs. R's shoes. No demur about their being 18s 11d, which she thought very dear. We seem to be in the Weymouth area for some villages and Poole for others but the line of demarcation is not definite. This is the most awful harvest weather. Met my cousin – very depressed without a field carried. No barley will be worth malting. He presented us with two leverets shot in the corn. They had shot 30 hares altogether and 10 in one field. He has all his sons and their friends harvesting for him.

Thursday, August 21. Took John for a picnic. I wanted to see the harvest and he remembered some goats we used to visit before the war. We met some school boys going back to Bryanston at 5 o'clock. They looked as if they had been working hard and nearly everybody had been carrying as it was a fine day at last. My Mother had been down to Bournemouth to see a specialist as she has recurring skin and eye trouble. He told her that she had been doing too much and gave her an arsenic tonic. She said Bournemouth was crammed and people were standing in queues for tea. I promised to mind the baby of Killicks while the rest of the family went cray fishing. I had never heard of it before they came and almost immediately afterwards we found one in an old tin. It rained too much to go.[52]

Friday, August 22. Sent on some posters which were sent to the WVS about fire in the cornfields. I should not think they need worry if the weather stays like this. Mrs. Stuart is worried about her sight. She has a cracked lens in one eye from a cricket ball. She has to appoint a deputy in case she is knocked out in a blitz. She has appointed the obvious person, who will be very nice to work for. A cousin came for a dance outside Salisbury. They knew the man at Camberley and his wife was nursing the small daughter with whooping cough so he asked her to be wife to him. She said her dancing days were getting over – her feet didn't last the night and she got so sleepy. It was so nice to [see] someone dressed up for once although she did not have a proper evening dress. She returned at 5.30 but had said she must be called as she had a batch of Land Girls who have been pulling flax in her neighbourhood to see off at the crack of dawn.

Saturday, August 23. The dance had been great fun. The flowers were a great feature as they had been done by two professionals who are now ATS. She told us about the complete failure of their jam making at present as there are only two big houses and she has given all her surplus to people who had saved a little of their own sugar. The

---

[51] 'Though they used thousands of gallons, Blandford firemen were hard driven to get a blazing giant hay rick at Mr. F.J. Brigg's farm, Littleton, under control during the early hours of Monday morning. The firemen were called at 1.45 a.m., Mr. Brigg having been warned by a woman who saw the blaze from her house. There were about 70 tons in the rick, and the blaze was seen as far away as Yeovil and Poole.' Eventually about half the hay was saved. (*Western Gazette*, 22 August 1941, p. 6.)

[52] Crayfish are freshwater lobsters, found in rivers.

Land Girls were a great success and no trouble. They turned out to be school girls from my own school.[53] There was an Australian among them who was extremely popular and had most incredible adventures. My husband rang up to say he would come down for the weekend.

16. Land Army girls in Dorset, 1944

Sunday, August 24. A frightfully wet day. It never let up once. Made a patchwork quilt for the Red Cross inspired by the *Picture Post*. Husband rang up to say the glass was still dropping and he would not risk wasting his petrol as he must look at the bees.

[53] Talbot Heath School in Bournemouth.

Monday, August 25. Lydia came in from Southampton for the weekend at home. She is enjoying herself at the training school. She shares a billet with another girl in a nice modern house a 3d bus ride from work. They had tests at first to see what they remembered of school and then they started on the machine making bolts and washers. It is much nicer than she expected. They pay 25s for their room and four meals and she earns 38s already and a further 3s each time they pass a test. There is no night work or weekends and they do week and week about morning and afternoon shifts so that she can come home every other week. Sorted out the most unspeakably dirty second-hand clothes sent in for the bombed. They look like workmen's coats and are far too dirty and greasy to store as they are. Chose out three or four of the best and decided to have them cleaned as we have none in the store and the rest must go to the matron's jumble sale for the hospital as she has said she doesn't mind what the things are as she knows she can sell them.

Tuesday, August 26. A cousin and her son of 10 here for one night. They have a house outside Dunfermline and she does Red Cross and all the other voluntary work while her husband is ARP and was Home Guard. She has five maids and doesn't know what to do. If she sends them away it means she can give up her voluntary work but it would also mean that she could not keep the various people she has who cannot find anywhere to live. They have a lot of Poles who had no idea how nice the English were until they lived over here and worked among them. Their idea seems that the hope for Poland is to be reconstituted under an English King.[54]

Wednesday, August 27. More bales of American clothing arrived for the clothing depot. No knickers or overcoats and we do need them so badly but they are so difficult for working parties to tackle. I wish we were able to distribute more but no doubt the time will come.

Thursday, August 28. Had mail from Australia. The three girls are settled at school and my sister has found a furnished house, rather like a seaside bungalow. She has a woman in from 8 till 2 and has to pay her 25s a week and give her dinner. She has bought the children bicycles so that they can explore at the weekends, and these were very expensive, but their uniform for school was not so dear as she expected. It is just like living in an American small town as shown on the cinema, and their arrival was noted in the local paper. She has met some proper residents that she was given an introduction to and has begun work at the local working party making pyjamas and pants on electric machines. Her nurse is a complete novelty.

The brewery has taken on the drying out of some of the farmers' corn before malting begins but the difficulty is the labour. It isn't easy to get a man who can turn a floor of grain evenly and his head maltster has had a slight stroke. Had a chat to the president of the local Bee Association and paid my subscription. She says a lot of people are keeping bees for the ten pounds of sugar and now they have to be inspected

[54] Many Poles settled in Britain after fleeing the Nazi and Soviet occupation of their country. Blandford Museum holds written testimonies from Polish refugees who were given support by the local people.

to see how many hives they really have.[55] Round Oxford they have been very careful from the beginning. Met the head of the jam making for S_____. She says they are getting on very well and the blackberries are coming and they have made a lot. Went to see the Ministry of Information exhibition at Sturminster [Newton]. Not a great success. Came home in a packed train with a batch of recruits from the Camp. The men who had come to fetch them looked very friendly and welcoming and the men seemed excited.[56] It is no longer light enough to type in the brewery office after dinner. I shall have to try and get it [the typewriter] on Sundays.

17. Regular soldiers at Blandford Station awaiting the arrival of conscripts in 1939

Friday, August 29. Sent out a circular to all WVS representatives on how to get coupon free wool to knit comforts for their friends. Got myself a boiler suit to do bees in with a zip fastener up the front. I shall be free of stings and it will do for fire fighting. I cannot get a long zip, only 12 inches. My husband got down for a night.

Saturday, August 30. A busy day with the bees taking honey. We have not done so badly with the ones on the farm and they were so good tempered for once.

---

[55] Some weeks later the secretary of the Dorset Bee Association claimed that, 'owing to the large increase in bee-keeping in the County, the work of the Association had been exceptionally heavy'. (Dorset History Centre, DCC: A16/1/19, County Agricultural Committee, Minutes of the meeting of the Agricultural Education Sub-Committee, 23 January 1942.)

[56] The following two sentences for August 28th are handwritten, as are all the subsequent diary entries up to September 23rd. Phyllis's handwriting is difficult to decipher, and Julian Walther, who had once laboured to read the letters his Mother sent him at boarding school, offered us his assistance and kindly made a transcription of these six handwritten pages. Our warm thanks to Julian for his help. Without it we would not have been able to master these entries.

Monday, September 1. John and I arrived at Delcombe for a fortnight. The new nurse seems most suitable – no frills or flowing talk and concentrates on the children. She is interested in unconventional ways of living so I think she would leave to go abroad after the war. Her last people went back to America but she was not allowed to go although his wife wanted her to go so that she could stay with her husband. The maid Thelma is trying to decide whether to volunteer or wait until she is called up. She is afraid of being sent to the ATS if she waits.

Tuesday, September 2. Discussed dances with Thelma (the maid). If there are any girls in uniform the soldiers always crowd round them so it is more fun when they aren't there, but the soldiers always advise them not to go into the ATS.[57] The village boys are so silly and won't learn to dance but all go to the dances and hang about and make remarks. Went out to tea and picked plums for the Women's Institute jam-making centre.

Wednesday, September 3. Picked more plums for the Women's Institute. John very happy because the thresher has come. My brother-in-law is selling the farm and leaving at Michaelmas so he threshes as he harvests, but so many people have had to do this with the wet harvest that prices may be difficult, or where they are controlled the dealers may not be able to take such big stocks. Picked blackberries after lunch.

Thursday, September 4. Made jam with the Women's Institute. Great fun on Primus's in shallow aluminium pans. Mine took a very long time. They did not take many stones out and the first lot were tied down cold but I expect it will pass. I disposed of the dog's puppy to one of the workers while we stirred. Made jam after lunch and picked blackberries. Took up jugs of tea to the threshers. It is either fetched or taken up every two hours and breaks into every occupation.

Friday, September 5. Went with my sister to the new house [in Higher Melcombe]. They are going in on the 15th but we must not start packing until the farm is sold and no one wants to see over it. Someone comes every day. They let the new house temporarily to some very unsatisfactory people in case it was taken for evacuees. The Home Guard have one room. These tenants are not going out until the weekend we move but they have very little luggage or furniture so we can have the sweep and the scrubbing done round them. They have two furnished houses let but have bungled all their arrangements and they have had to stay until the last possible moment. Salted down (runner) beans in the afternoon.

Saturday, September 6. The farm was sold to an old pupil's father, a retiring civil servant. The son will farm. All most satisfactory, a good price paying back what Peter gave and what he has put into it.

Sunday, September 7. Packed the china, glass and silver.

---

[57] The ATS at this time was ill regarded by many civilians (and some soldiers), mainly because of its reputation for loose sexual behaviour. This was almost certainly greatly exaggerated (if true at all). However, the Army, of which the ATS was a part, was notoriously given to swearing, which may have led some men to discourage women from joining.

Monday, September 8. Washing day. Picked blackberries in the afternoon. Made blackberry and apple jam. I read after supper. Peter has some soldiers to help with the harvest. No good at all until he said he would pay them direct and not the Government.

Tuesday, September 9. Made more blackberry and apple jelly. Chopped up apples for bottling. Picked blackberries. Took round the men's extra cheese rations.

Wednesday, September 10. Cycled to the village to cash a check[58] to pay the soldiers. Two lots working now, more experienced and good workers. The second lot bring their tea as well and have hard boiled eggs. I managed to get a half pound of chocolate at the shop. Chopped up apple again for bottling and for juice. Bottled carrots. Helped to pack clothes and medical supplies. Darned after supper.

Thursday, September 11. Fetched a wheelbarrow full of pre-war newspapers for packing. They will be much better.[59] Packed the empty jars and tins, jams and preserves. Packed books.

Friday, September 12. The threshers went – now we shall have the children under our feet all the time. Kathleen went into Blandford and I jugged the hare for her. An Esse[60] cooker is nice. Packed the pictures and mirrors, music and children's books.

Saturday, September 13. Washing day again. The incoming tenants have arranged to come in on Tuesday. What a mess and a mix up, everyone moving on the same day. If only Kathleen had not been in such a hurry after the sale it could have all been arranged so easily over a nice cup of tea.

Sunday, September 14. Turned out cupboards. Packed up kitchen china. I have had a wonderful offer of second-hand clothes from someone joining the ATS who has no place to store [them]. She offered them to my cousin for a jumble sale for the wool fund but she gave me first refusal as we are much the same build. Peter came home very critical of the Home Guard and the Sunday exercise. It is a frightful strain in the harvest and with the sale and the move on top of everything.

Monday, September 15. The incoming tenants are to stay the night so John and I have come home. Packed up to the last minute.

Tuesday, September 16. Back at the WVS office. Dealt with first issue of vouchers for coupon-free wool. The Red Cross head wants to pay our non-existing working parties a visit and make them keener on working.

Wednesday, September 17. Headquarters want to know about the Flying Squad of the WVS. Mrs. Stuart is sure it has faded out and must be stimulated. We have some

---

[58] She employs the American spelling here.

[59] Wartime newspaper was made from salvaged materials, due to shortages, and was poor quality.

[60] See note to 27 December 1941.

more applications for evacuee clothing. Picked blackberries. One crisis with awkward evacuees' case today. The evacuees have left them but the daily woman has another job so they are without help but peaceful. D. has been harvesting and that farmer had soldiers but they had to be fetched and so he found the volunteer labour more satisfactory. He was so happy being one with his fellow man instead of an outcast person. Kathleen rang up. The move was hell but they got in alright and the children are safely parked elsewhere until Thursday.

Thursday, September 18. Met the billeting officer who is going to Poole tomorrow and will see the Assistance Board about the needy family of evacuees. I hope they can have new American clothes which will last.

Friday, September 19. A friend of Mrs. Stuart came in with a small boy who was without a school as his had been commandeered at a week's notice. They had moved him from Winchester to Scotland so perhaps some Spitzbergen inhabitants are quartered there instead.

Saturday, September 20. My husband home for the weekend.

Sunday, September 21. We moved our bee hives from the farm here. No casualties but [it was] 10 o'clock before they were safely here. After we had nailed the travelling roofs on and were waiting for the bees to go to bed, we picked blackberries and nuts in the wood. It was the warmest, most summer-like weekend we have had. I wish he could have a holiday but he says it isn't worth having one unless they get him a deputy as he will have to do all the work when he gets back.

Tuesday, September 23.[61] Went to Bournemouth by bus. It was a lovely day and when we had bought our Christmas presents for India we went down to the sands with our lunch and spent the afternoon there. There were crowds of people still having holidays and looking as if they needed them. We came up in good time for the 5 o'clock bus and had a horrid tea and then queued for the bus. It is a scramble and almost impossible without help with parcels and a child. However we fought our way to the top and no one was left behind this time. They only run relief for the 7 o'clock.

Wednesday, September 24. Met Mr. Hunt, the town billeting officer, and asked him about some evacuees who want clothes and he suggested they applied to the Assistance Board so that we can give them new ones under the new arrangements. He said he had fixed up for a man to come and interview them but what he now wanted was furniture for some other families he was putting in requisitioned houses. I don't know of anyone but there must be some about. School has begun again at last for John. Mrs. Killick forgot to send Richard – in the throes of bottling at the Women's Institute centre. Very few people availed themselves of the scheme whereby they could take their fruit and bottles to the centre and have the syrup added and the sterilising done. More complications about coupon free wool. We must now put the number of ounces issued on the ration card as well as the voucher and endeavour to endorse their clothing card as well as the old ration book as there is nothing to prevent their taking their card

[61] Phyllis resumed her typed diary with this entry.

when they get it to the Women's Institute and registering for another 1½ lbs of wool with them.

Thursday, September 25. Headquarters now want all the tea chests and cases back that the clothing came in. We can't possibly store the stuff without a case or so. We also are to collect rosehips for their vitamin content. Spent the afternoon creosoting beehives. John started to help but preferred lifting potatoes with the gardener.

Friday, September 26. Hired the [honey] extractor but it was not big enough to do all the frames. Mrs. Killick came to help and the children got at the honey when they could. Richard was sick all over the drive. I wish I could have watched an expert on the job first but we got 30 lbs without getting stuck to everything. I cleared up after supper. Shooting has begun again[62] so we shall come off our diet of fish. There isn't much about now the price has dropped. There is not the game there was last year. They think people have looked for pheasant eggs to help out the egg shortage.

Saturday, September 27. Went on the downs while my Father visited houses to get some blackberries to send to London. Rather a disappointing expedition but nice to see the country people and the ploughing.

Sunday, September 28. Harvest Festival. I just got my honey potted up in time but I had to put it where the light would not show through it as it isn't nearly clear enough.

Monday, September 29. Sent out needlework to the working parties ready for the October drive – all pyjamas at present, which no one will grumble at, and knitting for the few who are not doing Dorset comforts. The British Restaurant is opening on the 8th and they want helpers. Asked the vet's wife who has no servants at present but said she would go one day a week. The hours will be 11 to 3 and your dinner as well. Mrs. Killick will do it after canteen the day her woman comes in to clean. Miss T. will do it too only she had infantile paralysis as a child so is not sure if she [can] manage it. The cases of food arrived for our reserve for the village in case of invasion. It all went into the attic easily and we thought it would be more bulky. The same two lorries had done the whole area and put some of it in cowsheds in some places. The sugar and tins of beans would be very easy to steal. My honey is in great demand. The schools are very short and mothers are wanting to send it for tuck boxes.

Tuesday, September 30. Got down a 'put-away' boy's bicycle from the attic to see if John could soon ride it and then I would not buy him a fairy cycle for Christmas. I have time to teach him now and after the war he will be sure to have to ride to school as we shall be in the country with the bees I hope. It was a great success. His legs are long enough if he has the concentration. It will save my life as I have had no luck about recovering my stolen bicycle. The police sent me on a wild goose chase to [Sixpenny] Handley where a bicycle had been sent in which answers to my description but was not mine. I shall have to buy another because I cannot ride my sister's mad nurse's any longer, especially as she is recovering and will need it soon. I went to look

---

[62] In Dorset the shooting is mainly for pheasant and partridge, and runs from 1st September to 31st January.

at it by bus and the front window had been broken by trees as they are not cut back as they used to be. I got a lift on a lorry on the way back but rather regretted it when I found my coat plastered with oil when I reached home.

Wednesday, October 1. A soldier's wife came for one of the American layettes. I must write to the welfare officer about her but I hope I can give her one. She seems rather easy going, not having a stitch ready and the baby due next month. She is living with her mother-in-law, a pensioner, and the house is unsuitable so she is going to a retired nurse's house and paying two guineas a week and paying it off every week now so she has not very much to spare from her 28s[63] if she is paying her board and keep as well. Met Mrs. T. who was very roused that at the Women's Institute meeting the committee had suggested stopping the W.I. vegetable stall in the winter because it would be so cold selling. She got her way.

Saturday, October 4. Mrs. Killick is going to stay the winter and has decided to buy a few more comforts to ease her country cottage existence. I have promised to lend her two beds and mattresses, some hair cord carpets and a comfortable chair. I have said I won't lend her anything I mind about as she does not want to have to pay for it and the children can't take care of things yet. We went to the second-hand shop in the town and looked round. There was a lovely oak settle which would just fit the house. She is toying with the idea of getting that but thinks she had better ask her husband.

Sunday, October 5. Cousins came to lunch and tea. He is a Colonel in the Army Service Corps stationed in Boscombe. They have been in Bristol and she worked in the WVS – in the crypt of a bombed church sorting all the Canadian and American parcels. She said there were heaps of boys' knickers so we were just unlucky. They have two children at school and have been living in hotels for 18 months but it is very difficult to get enough for growing children to eat and no extras, not being registered anywhere. Chocolates and sweets and matches were the worst and biscuits almost as bad. Instructions from headquarters to send in the name of any child who could not get Wellingtons locally and had to walk over fields to school and they would get Wellingtons from the American stocks. I can give that layette for 15 coupons so that is alright.

Monday, October 6. Went out to tea with my parents to meet a cousin[64] just been given command of a border regiment. He was in East Africa at the beginning of the war and missed his promotion as his commanding officer would not release him but now he is very happy and keen, especially as the regiment is being turned over to tanks. The 200 who will never reach the standard of intelligence required have been drafted out and the rest all doing courses. He was finding the actual learning very difficult as he never looks inside the bonnet of his car and was having to start from scratch, but the organisation and planning was the thing he was really enjoying.

Tuesday, October 7. Miss Harris came in for her weekly bath and told us about her getting the sack from the food office. It has been blowing up for so long and will be a benefit to her and all the rest of the staff, but the actual business sounded a bit

---

[63] This would have been her share of her husband's weekly pay.

[64] John and Julian Walther think this was Captain R.F. Woodhouse, (Rex), who lived at Larksmead with his sister Rita. He ended the war as a Major.

unsavoury. Major C. told her it was disciplinary action because she seems to have had a brawl with another girl over an ink pot and when she wanted to appeal to the regional office he told her he was the final authority. However, he let her put a call through and she has applied for an interview with them.

Wednesday, October 8. Fetched my new bicycle from the shop after depositing Kathleen's mad nurse's at the station. She is recovering now and thinks she has been bombed. The new one seems funny to ride and I have to lift my right foot so high to get on it as it has never quite recovered from being paralysed once. It does not seem to be as delightful as I expected. Still it goes very well and the brakes are excellent. I hope my old one turns up soon and helps to pay for this one (£6 10s). We had notice of a crate of dungarees that had arrived from America. How many would we like for our hostel, if any? I wrote and told them that the military had stepped in and taken the house we were going to make into the hostel but we should like 12 to keep in reserve. Spent the afternoon with Mrs. Killick picking her apples. At least the man from whom she borrowed the ladder picked all the high ones for her and the children wanted to pick all the low ones so I held baskets and children most of the time. We had a happy tea and came away in time for bed.

Thursday, October 9. Went to a picnic rosehipping. The T's wanted to make up their 28 lbs so three of us went with the children and two evacuees and made it up to 35 lbs. There are heaps about but they are not very nice to pick. In the morning I filed some of the aged letters from Mrs. Stuart's desk, which is a long job as the files have no springs and the letters are threaded on strings and once they are out of order it's a day's work to get them back. Every book is full of papers or notes so what would happen if she was struck down I cannot think as there is nothing in the files to help one. Took a parcel of baby clothes to a nice Mrs. W. who had come back from Shaftesbury with twin girls. She has a husband up at the Camp and an old father (still in work) and three older girls all in one of the slummiest houses but it was as clean as clean and she was only home a week. She was from Yorkshire and said the people down here were kinder to strangers than she had thought they could be. The twins were sweet but one cried at night and anyhow she did not get to bed till 12 with feeding them both. Miss Harris has got her interview and has been told she is only suspended until then so she won't be turned away with a week's notice. She is going to pour out an awful lot at her interview. I am afraid the authorities will end up on the Major's side. Got the extractor for tomorrow and a proper uncapping knife so perhaps I shall have dealt with the honey before the weather gets too cold after all. Mrs. Killick is going to come and borrow her bits of furniture.

Friday, October 10. There has been another row. The Stuarts have been removed from the command of the First Aid Post and the First Aid detachment has been told to take it on. This is what everyone has set out to be the arrangement from the beginning but when I said so to Mrs. Stuart when I first took on her job she said that the Medical Officer of Health had said the Red Cross ought to be independent and the town be responsible for the First Aid Post. They have always had to depend on the Red Cross for their personnel. Apparently they should have received a letter of thanks from the Town Clerk thanking them for all they have done but the County sent off theirs first so they just had the statement that they had been superseded. The

Commandant of the Red Cross had the same letter and as there was a practice that night they all had to meet without any preliminary work. The General read out the letter he had had and then said rather pathetically that nothing remained for him to do but to say goodbye and they went, leaving R. to it. She expected half the people to walk out but one tactful old thing said that they had all always felt that the Red Cross should have had the running of it, and then all settled down as if nothing had happened. R. told me all this beforehand but the Stuarts never mentioned it. Happily she did or I should have thought from the atmosphere that one of their sons had been killed. It is hardest on her really because she only went in as his second-in-command as he could not go down to the post in the dark alone (only having one arm) and she has done all the work because the aged military mind cannot deal with the small town mentality and she isn't a bit suited to the job. He ought never to have taken it on.

Dealt with honey all the afternoon and evening – 96 lbs from three of seven hives, which isn't at all good but we shall have cleared £5 profit which is not bad for the first year and all the experience I have bought with it. My sister Kathleen will probably let the house they are in now to a farmer who was bombed out of his farmhouse and has been living with small girls in the village pub for months. They want it so badly that they are willing to give up the drawing room for Kathleen to store the houseful of furniture and pay a furnished rent for it.

Saturday, October 11. Gardened hard to get the borders cleared before the weather breaks. Father went out shooting. He gets about three days a week although he is 77 but he says he is shooting as well as ever. John went to bed without tea complaining of a headache.

Sunday, October 12. John still ill – sore throat and sickness. Father looked at him tonight and said he would expect to see a rash in the morning and it was probably scarlet fever.[65] That has put the cat among the pigeons with the clothing depot in the spare room.

Monday, October 13. John miraculously recovered. He slept all night and was normal this morning. Mitch (our evacuee) took turns playing with him and I gardened until a soldier's wife arrived and said she still had heard nothing from the Assistance Board and the children had nothing warm. That makes a month since we put them onto the case. I said I could not give them new clothes without the Assistance Board but gave a second-hand outfit for each child. No top coats of course but I think they could get them themselves. We must have a clothing club they can pay into. It's the wives with husbands on the Camp who are the worst off I think – the men come down for supper instead of having it at the Camp and that is where the money goes.

Tuesday, October 14. John back at school again. We heard there were to be oranges for the children – it's a pity he is six so soon.[66]

---

[65] Phyllis's Father had trained as a doctor.

[66] The import of oranges by ship had become a trickle. Consignments were distributed sparingly, mainly through schools and clinics, to younger children. Children aged five and under received concentrated orange juice provided by the United States of America.

Wednesday, October 15. The quinces were picked in today – only three parts of a bushel but many of the people who used to wait for them have died out and no one will have much sugar to spare for jam so perhaps it does not matter. Last year we sold them as well as giving them away wherever we could. Went down to the T's and pruned their buddleias. When I got back I found it was the wrong time of year. Their book must be odd. R. rang me up to ask me to go to Welfare[67] in the morning so that I should know what the procedure is. I have joined to represent the village so that I can get a chance to know the mothers and babies. She told me that the Stuarts had been approached about giving up the First Aid Post. The Medical Officer went himself and saw the old man and when she came in in the evening she rang up and said that they both agreed to stand down. So rather a wrong impression was given but I suppose he could not think of a better way of breaking the news without having to make a speech.

Thursday, October 16. Went down to Bournemouth to see a friend and her husband who was on seven days leave after being an umpire in the battle. They had a nice room looking over the sea. It's a grand time for hotel keepers because they have put their prices up and cut the food down but their staff problems must be hell. He has not got his commission yet and is fed up, especially with the food, which he says will never improve until officers and men feed together. Directly a man shows any ability he goes to the officers' mess. It is not so bad at the battle station where the numbers are small (50) but at the depot where there are 500 in a big hotel they are quite unable to cope with bulk and the food is appallingly badly cooked. He also thought very poorly of his fellow men, the average being little higher than animals. His father, an artist, has got a permit to draw bombed London and is enjoying himself very much – if only he can place the stuff afterwards. His mother is working in the china department of Derry and Toms.[68] She must be over 60 but she said she was 50 and after the first week, which was terrible, she is enjoying it. The hours will get easier later on in the blackout. Elaine has got her old job back teaching domestic science in Kent schools. She enjoys it and gets well paid but finds a lot of difference in the different food offices. In one place she was sent a circular about children bringing blackberries to school, receiving 3d a lb for them and the centre being allowed sugar to make the jam and to use the jam in cooking. At another she had to fight tooth and nail to have the plan acknowledged and then was not allowed to keep the jam. Came home in the blackout. It is very easy going and coming now the holiday season is over.

Friday, October 17. I did wrong to help that soldier's wife with clothes. The Assistance Board had merely not bothered to advise either the billeting officer who had called them in or us and he had put them onto their own Society, who had helped them with new clothes and taken coupons from them. I still think I did the only thing in the circumstances and I hope they have coats now. The secretary of the Soldiers', Sailors'

---

[67] Infant Welfare 'was the maternity and child welfare centre where mothers could get advice on the ordinary day-to-day questions of their babies' feeding and general care. The clinics were run by local authorities or voluntary organizations and were staffed by health visitors and voluntary workers, and a doctor was usually in attendance. Mothers were encouraged by the health visitors to take their children to the centres for regular examination. Furthermore, most of the centres tried to attract the mothers by maintaining a friendly social atmosphere.' (Sheila Ferguson and Hilde Fitzgerald, *Studies in the Social Services* [London: HMSO, 1954], p. 146.)

[68] Derry and Toms was a department store on Kensington High Street in London.

and Airmen's Families Association here is an invalid in bed and her assistant is living six miles out so they can't be very active unless we tell them of the cases, which I hope we shall do now.

Saturday, October 18. John went over to my sister's for the day so I had the day off, or rather part of it as the car which gave him the lift over was late so we waited for sometime and watched the world go by. I gardened the rest of the morning and picked rosehips in the afternoon. I got on better this time – not so many stalks and 8 lbs in 1½ hours. R. rang up in the evening to ask for white elephants for her Red Cross sale. She also said she had got the ARP man to come and explain to the First Aid Post personnel what the reasons for the changeover were so that she would not have any stabs in the back if she could help it. He is new blood too and does not mind stepping on people's toes. She hopes they will not be quite so smug after this as there certainly are lots of ways in which they could be more efficient.

Sunday, October 19. Sunday school in the morning. Visit to the Killicks to see why they were not there and a nice cup of tea while John and Richard have fun. Home to do the washing before dinner. Rosehipped in the afternoon and playing with plasticine by the fire after tea like the proper winter.

Monday, October 20. We all went out to pick rosehips and blackberries – my Mother and Father and our evacuee. I forgot she was afraid of cows but happily she did not hear my Mother say there was a bull in the next field. There were plenty of blackberries although the country people used to say the devil spat on them on the 14th and they were poison after that.

Tuesday, October 21. Delivered notes round the town about Mrs. Stuart's meeting about emergency Rest Centres which she is having on Thursday evening. In the afternoon I finished off my 28 lbs of rosehips and did them up to send to Basingstoke.

Wednesday, October 22. The British Restaurant opened today with a free lunch to the local worthies – roast beef, cabbage and potato, jam puffs and a cup of tea. Mrs. Stuart pleasantly surprised. Collected the Red Cross opinions [about the British

Restaurant] in the afternoon as I delivered my white elephants at their stall. They all approved but would have liked bigger helpings. They were told that it [does] mostly stews with lots of vegetables in the ordinary way and second helpings could be had for a second ticket.[69] Someone had sent in some lovely knee rugs for sitting-out cases made from the pieces of the dressing gowns we made in the summer. They are feather stitched together and backed with sateen.

18. The former Parish Room, the first home of Blandford's British Restaurant

Thursday, October 23. Red Cross sale made £15 and were sold out by 1 o'clock except for plants and religious pictures. The new Mayoress is going to start a working party when she comes into office and wants 100 garments to make up.

Friday, October 24. My Mother's birthday – 69. Father gave her a new wheelbarrow and some shoe trees to replace the aluminium ones she gave to the War. I went to help get the room ready for the British Restaurant as it was Mrs. Stuart's day and one of her helpers had let her down. They had 150 children the day before but not so many were expected today. Mrs. Conyers the Mayoress had run it then and told us what to do but Mrs. Stuart did not like being told a bit. The interplay of personalities is fun. Mrs. Conyers had seen Poole where they do 400 and she said very few really have second helps and the organiser had told her to tell the servers to be sure to give the big boys a decent helping at the expense of the toddlers and old women. There seems plenty of room to have a queue and move along the counter. They have a canteen for the troops there every evening and the kitchen has been enlarged so it is really plain

[69] 'About seventy people enjoyed luncheon in Blandford's British Restaurant, when it was opened by Captain Angus Hambro, M.P. for North Dorset, on Wednesday' (*Western Gazette*, 24 October 1941, p. 3.) The parish room, after alterations costing some £400, was the site of this restaurant, which was intended to serve a hot meal of meat and vegetables, a sweet, and tea at a cost of one shilling (*Western Gazette*, 17 October 1941, p. 6).

sailing except that the larder is small and the coal stove which would be used if the electric failed is in a draught and the oven won't heat. Also the draining board isn't very large so that the washers up have to be helped. The girls from the brewery went down to it and said they liked it very much and were quite satisfied.

A boy in the Canadian Air Force turned up in the afternoon. He is the nephew of Mother's sister-in-law out there. He is 27 and the eldest of six; two of them are at school but the others are in the war effort, although people out there are not very war minded he said. He only landed on Sunday and went to Bournemouth and from there goes to finish his training, probably in Scotland. He asked how far it was from Bournemouth to the 'mainland' as he was surprised that the Government should put such expensive people as himself and the other trainees so near the German aerodromes. We liked him very much. They are in a hotel with 65 men to one bathroom and four of them have found digs out with better facilities for bathing.[70]

Monday, October 27. Mrs. Stuart rang up about the British Restaurant. The paid cook and one of the washers-up have walked out on them but they are going to manage with voluntary labour until they can replace her. The wages seem low – £1 a week of five days. She thinks it would be better to have the tickets taken at the top of the room so that the queue is under cover and there is no scrum in the lobby where the cooks are trying to carry in the food. Talking at the school when fetching John, the doctor's wife said she could not see that it would pay in this town so I was pleased to suggest that it was a way to get the next generation fed. I don't think it had occurred to her but she is a very good cook and manager herself so that her children would never go short on the rations. Picked rosehips to make some of this syrup myself. The ones I had already picked took so long to stew that I thought the vitamins must have been destroyed by prolonged boiling and threw them away. John is very thrilled because the men have come to point the brewery chimney. The weather has changed so they will have a miserable time.

Tuesday, October 28. I had a letter from headquarters of the WVS confirming my appointment as secretary of the Blandford and Rural Area and a lot about my duties and a month's notice – also the usual form to fill in showing that I am willing to comply with the Official Secrets Act. The whole thing is quite absurd and not at all what I agreed to when Mrs. Stuart said she thought she would have my position officially recognised, as I saw the documents that came to her. She got rather roused when I said I thought it nonsense as I am in no sense a secretary to the WVS but did just as much hospital work as anything else. She said she hoped that I would let her see anything I wrote to them and she hoped I would not tell them that we did no work here.

Wednesday, October 29. The doctor came to see the old General this morning. Mrs. Stuart had quite recovered from yesterday and agreed that I should return the Official Secrets Act signed but not the acceptance of my appointment in formal terms.

---

[70] Details concerning military accommodation in Bournemouth are reported in the booklet *Buildings and other Areas Requisitioned in Bournemouth during World War Two*, Bournemouth Library, U769.224. Around 30 sites, many of them hotels, accommodated Canadian military personnel during the war.

Thursday, October 30. I had a day off from the WVS so I went and dug Miss Harris's allotment. She has gone to the Bournemouth food office for a month to see how she likes it but as the manager of the National Provincial Bank has applied to my Father for her character she presumably does not mean to stay there. I borrowed a fork from an old man down there. He thought I was wasting my labour as she had not weeded or thinned out her crops but she will do better next year and she will have more time at the bank and won't be so worked up about her wrongs in the food office. It is perfect ground for digging with no rain for so long. I could get rid of the couch [grass] in another season. The town and rural food offices are going to be amalgamated and they are looking for a new head. Major C. has said so often that he was going to resign that he has really had to this time. I think the man who took his holiday for him took back a very bad report of the office so that and Miss Harris's row sealed his doom. I bet his wife would rather have him in an office all the week. Tried to buy a wedding present in the afternoon but could not get anything in the town. I supposed any stocks are being held for Christmas.

Friday, October 31. A large bale of material arrived at the WVS today for vests for men. It is the same stuff we had for shirts. It is to be an urgent order but we have had to fill the working parties up with pink flannelette nightgowns as this stuff has been so long coming. It will not be an easy job although they do not look at all complicated to make. Milton Abbas sent in a list of the Wellington boots they need for the children who have a long way to travel in muddy lanes and field tracks. Dorchester rang up about petrol returns so I was able to ask them about paying for them. Apparently they did not give away the fact that they were to be free in case there was a terrible rush for them but they are free after all on signing a yellow form. Milton Abbas had already said they would subscribe to the Red Cross instead so I hope nothing happens to dissuade them. Mrs. Stuart rang up in the evening to say that the British Restaurant was a frightful scrum. They had a meatless day with an awful lentil pie followed by boiled pudding and treacle and the treacle had not been warmed so it took ages to serve. Also she had been asked to seat the children and not let them come up for their pudding until they had all finished the meat. The consequence was the quick eaters were romping about and to crown all she got in a mix up with the money but it all straightened out when she got home and she was able to pay it in at the weekly meeting. The voluntary cooking has not been a success and they are advertising again. I suggested that I took it on if she releases me. It is a job I could do and the best for John and his holidays.

Saturday, November 1. Spent the morning writing to the WVS representatives telling them when the salvage collectors would call at their villages. The Rural District Council has given its mind to the collection of paper at last but it remains to be seen if the merchant will stick to his part of it. The Killicks looked in with our tarpaulin which they had to cover the load of furniture I lent her. We all went into the town when I had finished the ironing as she was buying a hat and was expecting a parcel of Wellingtons from Dorchester. Richard came back and played with John while I packed up Wellingtons for Milton Abbas where 13 children need them to get to school. They are to be free as they are American gifts but the parents who can easily afford it are giving a donation to the Red Cross. Went on making my pink nightgowns for the Red Cross after dinner.[71]

Tuesday, November 4. Sent out Ministry of Health's recommendations about gas precautions in Rest Centres. Apparently mustard gas cases might not be detected until the person had got through to the Rest Centres and they must be prepared to deal with it by taking them to the nearest bathroom and dealing with them there. All the villages have one house at least with a bathroom somewhere near the Rest Centre. The WVS may be allowed to issue clothing to people lending their bathroom so that they can clothe any cases which have to be treated. The clothing will consist of a union suit[72] for certain and nice warm sweater on the top as we have plenty of these to fit all. I must take a gas course this winter. The Killicks to tea. Went on with the nightgowns in the evening.

Wednesday, November 5. Sent out hospital bills all the morning and delivered some on the way down to school. John went out to the shoot to take some ale grains for the pheasants to keep them from straying so I had a free afternoon and finished off the nightgowns.

Thursday, November 6. Sent out notices in the morning. John stayed at school for dinner as I went for the first time to the Infant Welfare. It is held in the Congregational Hall on the first and third Thursdays in the month. My cousin Rita is the secretary and she does the records with someone to sort them out for her, while two others are weighing toddlers and babies and the nurse is conducting others to see the doctor.[73] They can have tea if they like and there is a stall with clothing as well as all the foods. It wasn't quite such pandemonium as I expected although the toddlers seem to hate their weighing machine, which was not quite steady, but there were plenty of toys. Some of my evacuee mothers were there, and the twins. Rita had to go off and meet a man from Reading who was to decide if the First Aid Post should be enlarged to a Point. They have the orthopaedic clinic up there now that the Red Cross are responsible and also a clinic for scabies every morning. Started a new line in depot garments – men's open neck short sleeve vests open all down the front. Very easy to make.

Friday, November 7. Sent out notices for National Day for Aid to Russia. Mrs. Stuart was very loath to have another one but we have done so many I don't see why she need mind so. Mrs. R. came in for some clothes for evacuees. One has a most unsatisfactory mother who sends rubbish not fit to put on him and then only at great pressure from the London County Council and the foster mother. I gave him out the essentials and they are going to get the forms filled in later. Her other family had run

---

[71] This entry was actually dated November 2nd, which was a Sunday. Since shopping would not have been done that day, we have altered the date to Saturday, November 1st. Phyllis's dating in the diary does not include the days of the week.

[72] A single garment for the body and legs, either an under or an outer garment. Also another name for the well-known 'siren suit', of the sort worn by Winston Churchill. Also known as a boiler suit.

[73] This cousin, Miss H.I. Woodhouse, known to Phyllis as Rita, was the Honorary Secretary of the Infants' Welfare Centre Committee. She lived at Larksmead (now a modern residential development on the north-west edge of Blandford) and had a warm friendship with Phyllis.

out of coupons so we fixed them up with second-hand pyjamas and pants and socks which will hang on until the New Year. It was a family of three boys with a splendid foster mother but she could patch and darn their things no longer. R's married sister has turned up again. She was discharged from the ATS and now has to take a job which will replace another girl. She has been up in Scotland with her husband and took a job in a butcher's shop mincing up the sausage meat. Carried on with the vests in the evening.

Saturday, November 8. Half term Saturday. We went to Bournemouth by train, which was a great treat, with R. his school teacher. It was her idea and great fun.[74] We had an hour in the shops and managed to find toys for my remaining Christmas presents but there was nothing there which was not very expensive. We had lunch on the front where the land mine dropped but it was all nicely cleared away and after that we went to the News Theatre for an hour. It was John's first initiation and he loved it, especially the *Silly Symphony*. We got back in time for tea.

19. Blandford Station

Sunday, November 9. Went to Sunday school and dropped in on the Killicks afterwards. Home in time to get the washing done before lunch. Played with John's proper bicycle after dinner and went for a walk. R. came in to tea. Father and Mother went to see *Hamlet* at Bryanston. They stayed to the end, which was 6.30. It shows how starved they must be of entertainment for Father to stay so long.

Monday, November 10. No school for John. Left him with our evacuee and went to WVS – sent out the notices I had typed on Friday. Went to tea with the Killicks and

[74] John Walther thinks this was Ruth Grundy, who taught before becoming a nurse and is remembered by both brothers as being great fun. See note to 16 Dec. 1941.

collected wood down the fields. Mrs. Killick worried because they do no handiwork now as some mothers complain because their children are slow learning to read and they concentrate on the three R's. R. went by as we were leaving so we discussed it with her and suggested they went on Monday afternoons and did clay modelling.

Tuesday, November 11. Did hospital work for Mrs. Stuart. Went and saw a soldier's wife who is having her fourth child in February and would like a layette. She is worse off than a lot of others and as her husband is putting in for an Officer Cadet Training Unit she has a drop in pay for a bit as well. She had not got her pint of free milk[75] and she wanted to go to the antenatal clinic so I was able to help her about that. More people want Wellingtons. John went to school again in the afternoon. It was his own idea as he hates staying to dinner. It is rather a trek to go so far again but it saves these awful walks in the afternoon which seem such a waste of time and it keeps him away from our evacuee who is aging perceptibly and finds him rather much. A huge dump of clothes for the depot arrived as we got back from school. Enormous number of second-hand shoes from America and more union suits of course. Mother and Father had a little jaunt and went off to Bournemouth to see the *Dancing Years*. Mrs. Killick rang up and told me that she went to retrieve a pram she had lent to a soldier's wife and was told by the woman's sister that a Mrs. Freak had come up to her in the park and told that Mrs. Killick had gone to Scotland and sold her the pram and took it away at the end of the week. Mrs. Killick and the sister went off to Mrs. Freak's house and took away the pram as she was nowhere about and told her son who was there who they were. The sister scrubbed the pram out with Dettol[76] and I hope they don't get scabies.

Wednesday, November 12. Material came from the depot in Dorchester for the working parties – 100 yards of grey flannelette for boys' shirts and 44 yards of thin stuff for women's nightdresses and enough stuff for three boys' overcoats. I brought pressure to bear on Mrs. Stuart to try out a new cutter-out and took the small bale of stuff down to her only to find that she was away. Cleaned my bicycle in the afternoon – that is the worst of a new one. Miss S., the headmistress, came to me when I fetched John to ask about nursery schools. Her landlady had been staying in Guildford and was inspired by their four most efficient ones to think that something might be done here as this is the only one anywhere round. She was planning to alter the barns with a grant from the appropriate authorities. I think it would be a grand idea but Miss S. does not really know what a nursery school is although poor R. has been trying to lead her in the right direction.

Thursday, November 13. Asked Mrs. Stuart if I could borrow literature on nursery schools for Miss S. She told me that Mr. Hunt the billeting officer was trying to get a house from the Army to establish a resident day nursery and hostel, so perhaps he could combine with Mrs. C. because she has the house and he has not a chance of wresting one from the Army. Mrs. Stuart very doubtful if a day nursery is a good idea as it will encourage mothers to neglect their duties! Besides, there is no work for them

[75] The distribution of milk was controlled by the Ministry of Food. Expectant mothers were allowed one pint of cut-price milk every day.

[76] A brand of disinfectant.

to do in Blandford, but the food shops will have to release some of their girls soon and there are plenty of daily places going which would augment the family income and put the mothers in daily contact with residents and they would get more friends. I felt for the first time I was of some use in the town, being able to link up the two sets of people. We are to investigate further the clothing club idea. I think it would be so convenient to do it in connection with the Infant Welfare as it is the mothers who have the trouble with saving and it would make them come. Went to help distribute point books but found that officers' wives had turned up and were very happy so I need not go or tomorrow either, which means I can have a decent weekend with my sister at Ansty. We had Colonel P.J. to dinner. Friends of his asked us if we would have him and his batman for ten days while he did a course but Mother could not face the extra cooking and there is no room for the batman. He was so nice and very keen on his regiment. He thought nothing of ATS as cooks and said the ordinary Army cook could manage the huge numbers very well but was hopeless with the small number in a mess. They managed very well on their rations until the young ones came and they cleared the board in five minutes and had to be lectured in the end. It reminded me of our students.[77] In Weymouth where he is stationed they have four British Restaurants all run by the WVS and the meals are so good that all the residents go and save their ration.[78]

Friday, November 14. Mrs. Stuart said she would be away on Monday so I could have had a long weekend but poor John came home from school feeling very low and only fit for bed so we stayed at home and he was terribly sick during the afternoon. I got a nice lot of my evacuee socks done while I read and sat with him.

Saturday, November 15. John in bed until tea time. Tried to get him a painting book in the town but there is hardly anything about. However, there will be a consignment of toys on December 1st. Tried to get a pair of pliers to go with his tools for Christmas but they were 4s 6d and very rough and heavy and it did not seem right to give them to a child when they are so scarce.

Sunday, November 16. John in bed for breakfast but much better. We stuck photographs in when he was up and then did the washing and he was happy with boats in the bath. I got my letters written afterwards and we walked in the fields after dinner. He had not much appetite but was glad to be out again and we saw a kingfisher fishing. We had an uproarious evening making a bear's den from the nursery furniture.

Monday, November 17. John to school and I had the day off so looked out for books in the loft for salvage and the troops. I found my husband's gramophone up there which he sent down for John. It was a great success but we have no decent records. We swept up leaves in the garden instead of afternoon school.

Tuesday, November 18. Issued wool permits. We go cheerily on without a hitch and then we get some person who seems to find it all incomprehensible. First she sends the

---

77 During the 1930s Phyllis ran a boarding house in London for medical students.

78 Dorset had one British Restaurant for approximately every 8,000 people, more than in most large cities. (*British Restaurants: An Inquiry Made by the National Council of Social Service* [London, 1946], p. 11.)

wrong ration books, then the right ration book without any margarine coupons in it, and finally instead of her clothing card she sends her small son's ration book. However, I call her up and find that he does knit so we issue him a voucher.[79] I sorted out all the chatty replies from the village representatives about salvage, gas cases, and Aid to Russia Flag Day. C[harlton Marshall] has refused to have a Flag Day but they come into Blandford so often that they can be asked to give then. S_____ cannot do anything about gas cases. The only bathroom is at the First Aid Post which has been told on no account to permit gas cases to pass through it and no one will take any training in dealing with it. Went to supper with Gay [Killick] to borrow her typewriter and had a lovely time. We had egg and bacon pie and Welsh rabbit and coffee and talked over our knitting by the fire. Our husbands and our children are so alike and we both find we make our own troubles. It is lovely to meet someone you can be friends with.

This entry marked the conclusion of another diary installment that Phyllis sent to Mass-Observation, and the following installment starts, unexpectedly, on the same day – 18th of November. Such uncertainties in dating are probably because she did not have a typewriter at home, and kept notes that she later typed up, at which point errors were liable to creep in. From evidence in her diary later this week, it appears that her first entry actually applies to 19th.

Wednesday, November 19. Went up to the WVS office and issued wool permits for coupon free wool for relatives in the Forces. Discussed the boys' shirts we are making from Ministry of Health stuff. They are using an American pattern, open down the front. Nurse said it would be simple to make it a little larger but she seems properly tied up now. I compared it with a Daniel Neal's[80] one of John's and found it was the same size and just what we want. Discussed starting a clothing club with Mrs. Stuart for the soldiers' wives – also a nursery school. She thinks it a great mistake

[79] It was not unusual for boys to knit as well as girls.

[80] Daniel Neal was a department store in Kensington High Street, London, which specialised in children's clothing, shoes and school uniforms. The business was started in 1837 and sold to the John Lewis Partnership in 1963.

encouraging mothers to neglect their duties and does not think they will be absorbed into part-time work in shops.

Thursday, November 20. Issued more wool permits. Unpacked parcels of needlework. Went to a sale of work in the Town Hall of work done by the Dorset blind. I used to buy beautiful socks for Christmas presents but three coupons kills that. I looked for bicycle baskets but they do not make them. Went up to the hospital to see my brother-in-law's uncle who is in there with a touch of pneumonia as he lives alone and has no one to nurse him. I felt I must as he has asked John and me to tea when I have been staying over there but he was not pleased to see me at all so I need not go again. Went up to a gas lecture. It's all in the book but it was a good thing to go and hear it.

Friday, November 21. Enquired at the draper's about clothing clubs. There is one very strong one which gives you 2s 6d in the pound if you leave it in 12 months and they call on you every Monday and you pay in what you like. They also have a hire purchase system but that is only for permanent residents. We could not do anything better than this and they have the biggest stock of clothes anywhere round here so that will be the end of that. Went to help at the British Restaurant. It does not run very smoothly. The supervisor cannot supervise and is difficult to work with. The voluntary cooks found that she would not tell them what to do, put the groceries out, and leave them to get on with it, and now that scheme has stopped and she helps an old cook do it all with two young women to wash up and do vegetables. I found, myself, in our boarding house that if you do the cooking you are on the kitchen side against the dining room, and it is just the same here. They run the dining room short of potatoes rather than go short themselves and when her pals come in she tells the servers to give them an extra big helping. They seemed pressed with the washing up so I lent a hand out there and could see what it was like. They made the tea too without boiling water, which seemed infamous. I stayed for lunch and had the 1s worth which was good and well cooked but I felt like bringing my own knife and fork after seeing the standard of washing up. They have a grand boiler but for some reason the water has to be baled out instead of using the tap and this seems to require great economy in water.[81] Took Wellingtons round to the village school for children who have rough walking to school. Being American gift stock they cannot be sold to the mothers but we point out that we will accept a donation to the Central Hospital Supply Service depot and they all give a little something and the richer ones give the full price. My husband rang up and said he would try and get down on Saturday.

Saturday, November 22. No sign of J.R. all day. I made one of the little shirts up to see how they went and to see if my directions were adequate. The stuff is rather thick for small children but nice to make up. The Killicks came to tea. No fights and very peaceful and happy.

---

[81] Blandford's British Restaurant struggled to succeed, and during its first six weeks of operation served little more than 1,000 meals to adults. 'An increase in the number of adults using the restaurant was hoped for, but time would be needed to break down prejudice. Councillor J.E. Conyers [the Mayor], a regular patron, humorously offered to dine there in his robes of office if by doing so he could persuade the general public to make more use of the communal feeding centre.' (*Dorset County Chronicle*, 4 December 1941, p. 2.)

Sunday, November 23. J.R. turned up after all. Very optimistic about Russia. Cheered me up by saying I need not worry and there would soon be plenty of jobs even down here for mothers. He won't be down for Christmas but might get longer before or after.

Monday, November 24. Day off because of J.R. but he went off soon after 10. Did his washing. Delivered some more Wellingtons. Started my sister's mending. Her husband has been in bed and she has to read to him and this was the accumulation of weeks. She wears her stockings far longer than I do. It was a judgement on me for my extravagance.

Tuesday, November 25. Undid needlework parcels. [Iwerne] Steepleton seem to be in trouble over the wool I sent them but she found the directions in the end. But I had sent Shroton [Iwerne Courtney] more than I said on the invoice. They do the wool up in different amounts and the hanks were 12 ounces instead of 8. Mrs. W. came in in the afternoon and told me all about a long case which should be dealt with by the welfare worker and the secretary of the Moral and Spiritual Welfare, but she happens to be almost senile and bedridden and makes trouble, so what is the thing to do? She meant to see my Mother but Mother was so sure that she wanted me about clothing that I heard all the story before I realised the mistake. It is appalling that we have no active welfare worker here, but the Moral and Spiritual Welfare have no money and the County do not seem to think it necessary. If you go and see Miss W. in bed it is just like going down a sewer. She tells you details of every sordid case and you never find out what you came for so most cases just drift.

Wednesday, November 26. Bales of stuff arrived from the Personal Service League. They lost our order just when we promised the new Mayor's wife 100 garments to start a needlework drive within the town and now they have sent the order in duplicate – £30 worth – but we have a little more money than we had. The stuff gets worse and worse. Went to a memorial service for Mrs. B. in our village. Everyone said she was very nice but she never did much in the village except give a subscription when she was asked. She had appendicitis and died suddenly when they were hoping she would get over it. He nearly died of pneumonia last year but they pulled him out of the grave with EMB[82] or whatever it is and he took on the MFH.[83] The service looked like a meet afterwards on the green outside the church. All the hunting crowd were there but in black.[84]

Thursday, November 27. Typed out directions to send out with the garments to make it as foolproof as possible. Gave another pint of blood. Not such a good doctor this

[82] She means M and B, a drug supplied by May and Baker. Founded in 1834 in London, the firm had a breakthrough in 1937 with the development of M&B 693, an early form of penicillin, which could treat bacterial pneumonia, hitherto a killer.

[83] Master of Fox Hounds.

[84] The local press provided a detailed account of the death of and memorial service at the Church of [Blandford] St. Mary for Mrs. Katherine Beever, wife of Major Henry Holt Beever, of Littleton House. She 'had been a keen follower of the Portman Hunt, of which Major Beever is joint master with Mrs. W. Percy Browne.' (*Western Gazette*, 5 December 1941, p. 3.)

time. I think I put her off and she dug into the wrong part of my arm so I had a nice cup of tea while that settled down and then she had another shot in the other arm although she tempted me by suggesting that I went home. I loathe the whole process.[85] I had a nice cup of Oxo[86] the next time and got home at tea time and then dashed off to the gas lecture but the room was frightful with 40 people and no air and I had to come out before the end. Such a to-do. I might have just as well have fainted quietly on the floor. Most people seem to have felt it more this time. Our Rachel was done for the first time and she had a headache and a weak arm and Mrs. Killick complained that her arm felt strapped up too much.

Friday, November 28. Met Mrs. Ky. In the fish shop. She brings in a little workman's blue can for her fish and carries it very easily on her bike. I asked her if G. was too big for her carrier seat yet and would she think of me when she was. She said she was nearly and she would give it to me. Asked about Clayesmore Prep[87] where G. is now and they have a mixed first class. She said the new mistress was wizard with them. The fees are £8 8s which seems a bit stiff but I should like John to have a good start and he can't stay to lunch in a crisis at the Grammar School. Met Mrs. C. and talked to her about nursery schools – she is very keen. Went with her to find Mr. H. She was rather diffident about seeing him as she had a row with him about his fish but he is not a bit like that. He was out so we had a cup of beastly tea and waited for him to come back and discussed schools. Bryanston is starting a prep in conjunction with an evacuated prep in their buildings under an old master of theirs so she will send me the literature. Her husband is a master there and produces all the plays. Went back to Mr. H. but he had gone out again. Chased him to the British Restaurant but missed him so Mrs. C. decided to write to him. Went to my sister's for the weekend. She was temporarily in a house belonging to my grandmother that we stayed in as children. It was never designed for a family of small children and all the romance has quite gone now. We see it from an adult's point of view.

Saturday, November 29. A nice Mrs. Kw. came to tea.[88] They are moving into the house when Kathleen moves out. Their farm was bombed and now they are living in the village inn and the military have what is left of theirs. The furniture they stored away in it has been ransacked by the soldiers and the cat was being fed on one of her best soup plates. Two antiques had been removed altogether so she suspected that someone who knew what they were doing had looked into it. They had the Land Army girls but not properly trained. One was London Irish and worked when she thought she would and the other was an artist who found it all very difficult and minded losing her beautiful hands. They had also had the Army working for them but only one man was any good. They did not bring their rations the first day so she contrived a dinner

---

[85] It was proudly reported that 203 people from Blandford and district gave blood on this and the previous day (*Dorset County Chronicle*, 4 December 1941, p. 2).

[86] A cube of dried beef stock, used for gravy or as a warm drink.

[87] Clayesmore School was founded at Enfield in 1896 and moved to Iwerne Minster in 1933. A Preparatory School was started in Charlton Marshall in 1929 by Mr. R. Everett, and was taken over by Clayesmore in the late 1930s. The Prep School joined the main school at Iwerne Minster in 1974.

[88] John and Julian Walther think this may have been Mrs Kellaway, who lived at Bere Regis and rented farm land at Ansty.

for them and after that they always left them behind but her husband was told to claim for the meals provided. She had four girls to educate and was finding it difficult to find schools but she had a sister in Dorchester and they could stay with her and go as day girls.

Sunday, November 30. Went to lunch with a cousin. She is driving a mobile canteen twice a week taking meals out to three schools in the rural area round Dorchester.[89] The only trouble is that the containers are so heavy and some of the helpers have had to give it up. At the third school they help to serve it out and they collect up the empties on the way home. The school provides the plates and does the washing up.

Monday, December 1. Typed all the morning. The town Rest Centres are to be inspected and the rural ones are encouraged to have periodical get-together meetings to promote esprit de corps. Crashed into John's trike on our way to school. I stopped to talk nursery schools to Mrs. C. and instead of going on John came back to see where I was just as I was turning in at the school. I buckled his front wheel but did not hurt him. I took the wheel to the shop and he thinks he can straighten it in a few days. Met Rita at the Red Cross room to fix the tins for the Flag Day for Russia. She brought a dog which surprised a cat in the room and it shot straight through a closed window. We dashed to the window but there was no sign of the cat or blood – only masses of glass everywhere. It really is true that they have nine lives then. Rita is secretary of the Infant Welfare and said the town clerk had asked them to run a day nursery but they have no personnel and no buildings. She had been to Dorchester as referee in a gas exercise. It was most interesting but she was surprised that quite elementary mistakes were made by people who should have known better.

Tuesday, December 2. Mr. H. wants day nursery for evacuees and is not keen on the nursery school for all and sundry but Mrs. C. is still full of hope and showed me plans of the buildings and how suitable they would be. The flags had come so I joined R. and Mrs. T. to get everything ready to send to the villages. R. told me a woman had applied to her to drive the ambulance and made out she was used to blackout and held a licence and it turned out that she was learning to drive and wanted a vehicle with petrol to learn on. Mrs. T. told me that her sister had been staying in Frome where she helped at the nursery. It was beautiful and she said to the nurse in charge, I suppose these children's mothers are working in the factories, and the nurse said that they were not because the nursery opened and closed an hour later and earlier than the factories. The sister was also very put out when she went to collect some rents to find one of the children's mothers a lodger in one house and doing nothing for herself or anyone else while voluntary workers were making time to help her.

Wednesday, December 3. Advised all the representatives that the flags etc. were ready for them. Helped at British Restaurant. I was quite redundant but Miss C.S. likes to have shoals of workers. The school children did not come in such a rush so the adults

---

[89] This was Stella Woodhouse, wife of Brigadier Charles Woodhouse. They lived at Higher Melcombe. Stella's daughter remembers the mobile canteen being decorated with jolly animals, to the delight of the hungry schoolchildren (information from Julian Walther). The mobile canteen delivered school meals to rural areas. Meals were prepared centrally and sent out in vans.

20. A Gas Exercise in Dorchester, April 1941

were able to have tables to themselves. The children seem to clear their plates better now and are used to the food. Some of our village children were there. I came home to dinner, which is much better though not such fun. I got into the attic and was able to look among my nieces' put-away toys for the train set I am buying from one of them for John. I looked up what its present value is and it would cost £2 11s as against 24s. Fetched John from school. The headmistress is in trouble about the extra coupons for her big girls.

Thursday, December 4. John told me he was supposed to take toys to send to Russia. I felt this was really the last straw, with toys so precious, and books would be no good, but happily I met his teacher who said it was only for a toy stall in Aid of Russia so he dug out two books in nice condition. Looked up about coupons, and she has to apply to the County Education Officer, and she has until the end of term so there is no need to fuss.

Friday, December 5. Packed up the 100 garments for the Mayoress. Most of them straightforward so I do hope I do not have to remake any of them. Finished stocktaking in the clothing depot and sent off the lists.

Saturday, December 6. I had the doctor to see John. He always seems to have a pain or be feeling sick and eats nothing at all. He [the doctor] says he is growing too fast and has a sluggish liver. I am not to give him more than a pint of milk a day or two ounces of butter a week and he is to start the day with soda bicarb. He must have his shoes built up still more for his flat feet and not go to school in the afternoon. It does not seem at all a difficult programme to carry out.

Monday, December 8. Had a letter from Australia. My letters by sea get there as quickly as the air mail. She says they have no direct taxes at all out there for the war

– all the money is being raised by loans. But the petrol rationing is very strict and the tradespeople cannot get their supplies through. Her nurse has volunteered for the Women's Auxiliary Air Force, which will be a great loss but a saving financially.

Tuesday, December 9. There is to be an ATS recruiting drive throughout the County. The village representatives are asked to deliver leaflets and advertise the exhibition and film at the Town Hall. Typed the preliminary notices. Gay came to supper and we went to *Target for Tonight*. The first film was rotten and we wished we had stayed at home longer where could talk but we both enjoyed *T for T* very much indeed. We both bought packets of plain chocolate which you cannot get elsewhere.[90]

Wednesday, December 10. Aid to Russia Flag Day. We collected today but the town has theirs tomorrow and some of the villages next week. Only three places wanted to change the number of flags and boxes sent out to them. Of course there was a muddle about the one person who makes difficulties. We did not do very well because it is too dark to get much done before school and after dinner everyone seems to be out.[91]

Thursday, December 11. Went down to Bournemouth in the car to finish our shopping. It was a treat. We ate our lunch on the way and called in on an uncle's[92] bungalow to leave him a present of jam and honey. He is over 70 but got into a munition factory after some trouble and works at a lathe as he did in the last war, but then he was near Basingstoke and had a chicken farm as well. Toys were very scarce and expensive but happily I had bought all the ones I wanted. We got back to find Miss Bennett from the prep school had come in to see me. John took to her at once and she seems very good and the hours would fit very well if the F's could bring him back as far as their house. She suggested that I came down to look at the school in the morning and I could do that as Mrs. Stuart goes down to the British Restaurant and there is not much to do. Left it open.

Friday, December 12. My little plan did not work because Mrs. Stuart had a very bad cold and did not go to the Restaurant and a lot of photographs came for the exhibition with their captions stuck to the back so they all had to be copied and put in front. There is no hurry about the school, though, because I must give a term's notice and I should like him to finish learning to read with Richard. Went for a walk with John. They have ploughed up a bit of down that has never been done before. We watched the tractor. Packed up honey and wrote Christmas letters.

Saturday, December 13. Turned out the toy cupboard and found some toys to give away. Went up to the post office to get out clothing cards. Went down to see the Killicks with a toy the children could play with alone and found that Father Christmas had arrived at an art and craft house very near. We joined them and I borrowed some money. The whole village was there and we were a bit late. One room was packed with

---

[90] There were at this time two cinemas in Blandford, the Palace and the Ritz, opposite each other on East Street.

[91] This flag day 'in support of Red Cross aid to Russia held at Blandford and the rural districts raised £135 1s 5d'. (*Western Gazette*, 9 January 1942, p. 2.)

[92] Julian Walther thinks this was Frederick Witt, brother of Phyllis' Mother.

possible presents and the other had three strings stretched across – 6d, 9d and 1s – with trifles attached. Father Christmas was Mrs. Oliver with a hideous mask which was not well received by junior members. John chose a model aeroplane made by a nephew of Mrs. Killick from wood – rather expensive at 9d when it was about two inches long and too frail for a child to play with. Went up to Bryanston in the evening to a concert and to meet the H.M. of the prep school.[93] My sister turned up and we all went round as prospective parents but they do not want them younger than 6½ and they must read. It seems a wonderful system for bright boys at all events and Mrs. C. is a great enthusiast and made it sound marvellous.

Sunday, December 14. Too wet for Sunday school. Did the washing and packed up parcels. Went to tea with the Killicks. Met R. who staggered me with a scheme of hers. She has heard of a resident day nursery at Shillingstone where they want a teacher for the 2–5s. She must sleep in and take night duty sometimes. Apparently she is paid by the month and can give John's headmistress a month's notice and she is very unhappy there as they have no idea what a nursery school is and only want the children brought on to read as quickly as possible. The other two members of the staff are not at all nice to her. She goes for the interview on Monday. This rather alters my plans for John. I shall have to move him next term unless he has two changes running – and what about a term's notice?

Monday, December 15. Mrs. Stuart better. Did wool permits and parcels. Posted most of my parcels. The post office very full. Had John's hair cut.

Tuesday, December 16. Sorted out socks into their sizes at the WVS ready for packing. Saw Ruth Grundy[94] again and heard more about her proposed job with the resident day nursery. They are rather rushing her into it as she is so keen and want her to sleep in. Her housemate may be called up as a masseuse in which case she would be better living in if it did not mean she had a lot extra put on her which she isn't capable of doing.

Wednesday, December 17. Mrs. D. applied for footwear for a family of five in her village who had been interviewed by the Assistance Board. She disapproved of charity for them strongly. There will always be jealousy of evacuees and all they get in the villages. Typed out directions for making balaclava helmets for some nice new wool that has come from the Red Cross. John broke up school. Ruth has got the job. I wrote to Miss S. saying I would take John away this term instead of next to avoid changing teachers twice.

Thursday, December 18. Infant Welfare in the afternoon to take the place of one of the doctor's wives. I am to go always in future to take Mrs. B's [place] as her maid has

[93] Head Master.

[94] This is one of the few occasions when Phyllis gives a person's full name. Sometimes it is clear that a person identified as 'R.' in the diary is Ruth, sometimes it is clearly Phyllis's cousin Rita; in these circumstances we have supplied the name in full. When it is unclear who 'R.' stands for, we have refrained from guessing. Ruth Grundy was the sister of Peter Joyce's first wife, who had died in childbirth. After Peter's marriage to Kathleen Woodhouse, Ruth continued to be friendly with Peter, his new wife, and their family.

been called up and she has three children. Went down to have dinner with Gay to meet the rector and his wife. We had soup and mock goose[95] and apple fool and we talked about making cider.

Friday, December 19. Ruth Grundy had her party for her form. Kathleen was coming too and bringing Thomas and the milk but she did not come and did not come, and just when we had decided on cocoa with water, she arrived, having had a breakdown. Kathleen did her shopping and came in to a [word missing] so we discussed Christmas and how many presents she was going to bring in for the children to have on the tree so that I should [bring] about the same number for John. J.R. rang up in the evening but the line was so bad we could not talk at all. He might come at the weekend.

Saturday, December 20. Gay and the children to tea. Her ceiling had come down in the cottage but they were going to put it up for her before Christmas. Her husband had been able to get a Meccano[96] for John in Harrods.

Sunday, December 21. J.R. did not come after all. It was his birthday so it would have been nice. Went to Sunday school with John and a walk up the Camp road in the afternoon. It is very wide now but with nice puddles for the tricycle to go through.

Monday, December 22. Packed up parcels at the WVS. Met Gay in the afternoon coming into town to try and get a key mended as the children had wrenched off the door of a cupboard and broken the key. Mother went through all her spare keys and we found three that might do. Meanwhile she took the broken one into the ironmonger's. When she came back she had met a woman who had kindly told her that if she wanted sweets she should go to certain sweet shop and say to the girl 'Have the fruit drops come in yet?' and she would be able to get some, but apparently if you walk in and say 'Have you any sweets?' they know you are not one of the chosen and you go without.

Tuesday, December 23. Not much doing at the WVS. We exchanged presents. I gave her a pot of honey and she gave me a tin of Lyons sweets for John. Gay had a lunch party for the children as they have lamps and it is impossible to see the children back in the blackout. I took John down at 12 and saw the other six arriving. Went and saw an old friend in the town and packed up presents. We had presents from India. Mother had butter and cheese and we had chocolate. Very expensive and very stale. The Army and Navy out there seemed to have muddled the order because all the tickets were mixed up.[97] We had someone else's tea and the cheese was addressed to me but we knew what we were having and sorted it out.

---

[95] There are several recipes for mock goose, which was a baked dish containing potatoes, onions and cheese with stock and herbs, but sometimes with additional ingredients if available.

[96] A popular toy comprising metal rods and other components, which screwed together to make toy vehicles, cranes, bridges, and a host of other things.

[97] The Army and Navy Stores offered a gift service. On receipt of a list of presents required, with addresses of recipients, they would pack up and dispatch gifts on behalf of customers.

Wednesday, December 24. Church decorations and house decorations. John spent a happy time delivering in the van, only they had two punctures and were very late for lunch, but I rang up Kathleen who said they had called in there and mentioned a puncture. J.R. rang up in the evening and arrived that night.

Thursday, December 25. John woke up at 5 but went to sleep again till 6.30 when we opened stockings. He is still a firm believer and staggered me by bursting into tears at the end, saying I had not given him anything. Went to Sunday school with him. J.R. had breakfast in bed. Kathleen and family arrived at 12.30 – three children and nurse and husband. Our pet evacuee came down and we were a proper family party. J.R. coming made Christmas. We had turkey, plum pudding and mince pies. Dessert was poor but Isabel had sent us some figs from Australia and Mother soaked some prunes and we still have nuts and apples. There were crackers and sweets. Afterwards nurse and the children went for a walk. The men talked and we had a nice gossip round the fire until the Christmas tree. J.R. retired to bed then and we had the tree and then tea, which I roused him for later on. Then they all went home and J.R. and I had the fire to ourselves in the drawing room and the extra wireless on an extension and it was just like having a home again.

Friday, December 26. John happy playing with new toys. J.R. read all the periodicals he had missed until it was time to go and he dropped me in at the British Restaurant for an evacuee party on the way.[98] Most of those invited turned up but they were mostly mothers and young children as the unaccompanied children have gone in increasing numbers. The menu was soup and rolls, roast beef, baked and boiled potatoes, sprouts and Swedes, plum pudding and mince pies. All the children put their rolls into the vegetable soup, after which they had room for a mince pie and nothing else, but the town did not want to be mingy so they had all the rest and a lot of it was wasted. After it was over they went to a free show at the pictures and back again to a tea but we did not help with that. We were treated to a spread for our lunch – turkey and all the rest – if we could have eaten it, but most of us took our plates out and insisted on having less. I walked back with J.T. who looked in to see *Country Life* and the *Illustrated London [News]* we had for the day. John and I went on with her and I looked at our beehive down there to give them a little feed as it continues so mild.

Saturday, December 27. John and I went to Kathleen's for the weekend as she wanted to take a day or two off. It was the first time we have stayed in the new farm. She has no spare room so we stayed with a cousin in the same village. The new house seems very nice and there are plenty of fires – log fires in the nursery and sitting room, an Esse cooker in the kitchen, a Beeston in the changing room for the hot water, and a coal fire in the dining room with a Cook and Heat.[99]

---

[98] Earlier in the month there had been a discussion at the town council concerning 'the proposed Christmas entertainment for evacuees in the borough. Funds for this purpose will be raised in part by a grand whist drive'. (*Dorset County Chronicle*, 4 December 1941, p. 2.)

[99] Esse were a Swedish firm which manufactured cast-iron ranges, originally wood-fired but later fired by coal. A Beeston was a hot water boiler made by a company called Pearson in Nottinghamshire. A Cook and Heat was an open fire with an oven installed above it.

Sunday, December 28. Kathleen and Peter went to Devonshire taking Nannie, whose people live in Taunton, so she was dropped on the way and Thomas and the baby. I was left with two and we had a blissful day.

Monday, December 29. There was no water in the house so we could not do washing before Kathleen went to London. They are very short of water because there was so little rain but there is an electric pump which will save our lives. It all sounds very complicated but when they have gone off I expect someone will help and Nannie is very unruffled. The maid has gone down with a feverish cold and I don't know where anything is.

Tuesday, December 30. Got on all right. Nannie remembered where the potatoes were kept and fires all kept in. She is 33 and due to register in February. She did think of leaving and getting into a day nursery but Kathleen needs her so much that she thinks she will risk it and stay and if they do call her up she can still get into nursery work.

Wednesday, December 31. Kathleen got back all right. I had got the washing done but not the ironing. They had enjoyed themselves and she spent some money buying forward for the children at D.H. Evans sale and shoes for herself at Babers.[100] We took the children to a party in the village for all children. It was suffocating. Oil lamps and an impenetrable blackout system. They did not join in very much because the big boys

[100] D.H. Evans was a department store in Oxford Street, London. Babers was a chain of shoe shops.

had a lovely time sliding up and down the floor. The little ones went home early but John insisted on staying and seemed to like it. They all had National Savings Cards with a stamp instead of little presents.

Shortly after Phyllis wrote this entry, most of Blandford's iron railings were removed. According to the Dorset County Chronicle *of 1 January 1942 (p. 6), 'The list of those which will be retained is very small. Just over 130 tons are scheduled for removal, and those which are being held back will remain either because their retention is justified on artistic grounds or for reasons of safety. The beautiful hand-wrought gates which form part of the Grammar School war memorial will stay, and so will the elaborate example of the art of the craftsman in iron which forms the entrance gate to Dale House in White Cliff Mill Street. The Shamble railings will go. The protective railings at the bottom of the gardens which skirt the Ham and Marsh will be left untouched, and so will the railings surrounding the areas of houses in North Place. In each case where the railings are to stay their absence would involve risk to life and limb. Of the twenty-odd appeals which were lodged the majority were dismissed.' Blandford's streets, the writer thought, 'will present an unfamiliar appearance. The town will look more spacious; some of the streets a little wider.'*

1942

Thursday, January 1. Came home. Ethel has gone into the milk factory[1] so I get up and make myself a cup of tea at 6.30, read to John until 7, and then go down and do her work, but Mother lays the breakfast while I get John up. After breakfast I make the beds with Rachel and do the bedrooms before I go up to the WVS.

Friday, January 2. Made out lists of the needlework done by each village to publish in the *Western Gazette*.[2] Had a small boy to clothe. He seems to be billeted with evacuees and to have been in hospital and come out with very little. I gave him a suit, sweater, vest, stockings and boots. He had an overcoat of sorts. I hope the billeting officer will succeed in getting me the coupons.

Saturday, January 3. Did the passages and stairs – quite like being at home again. Went down to have a look at some bees in the afternoon and met Ethel. She had survived a day and a half at the milk factory. The first day she had worked in the powder room but the next had worked in the open unloading and loading, which was very heavy. Also met E. Harris, late of the food office, and now in the Midland Bank. She had again a grievance, thinking she had been got there on false pretences as there was not enough work for a speed typist and the manager was trying to turn her into a cashier. She was sticking her toes in.

Sunday, January 4. Sunday school, and then cooked the dinner and did my washing. It turned out alright but the gravy seemed a bit thin with not much fat to baste the joint.

Monday, January 5. Typed out lists of the work done for the Red Cross by the different villages so that we can make an announcement in the press. Did up parcels. John and I went up to my cousin Rita so that she could get out and see her personnel for the First Aid Post. She has her cousin there who is dying of cancer and waiting to go into a nursing home. She has suddenly got bedridden just when the maid has got married and is away for her honeymoon. She is coming back but as her husband lives in a nearby village and works on the roads it sounds like a very temporary arrangement, unless the honeymoon is a complete failure.

Tuesday, January 6. Went up to Rita again until midday. John frightfully cold on the trike getting there so early and in tears when we arrived.

---

[1] The milk factory opened in 1888 at Bailey Gate, near Wimborne and produced milk and cheese. It was later taken over by Unigate Dairies. Milk production ceased in 1978 and cheese processing finished in 1989 when the factory closed. (*History of Sturminster Marshall*, W.H. Coomer, 2008.) Ethel would have travelled to work by train from Blandford.

[2] No such details appear to have been printed in the *Gazette* – at least not in the edition for North Dorset.

Wednesday, January 7. Sent out bills for the hospital and indexed the ledger. Sent out parcels of needlework. Had an application for clothes for a small boy at [Tarrant] Hinton whose parents provide nothing. Sent him an overcoat, knickers, socks, pants and two union suits.

Thursday, January 8. Had a field day in the clothing depot room and got it all straight. The union suits were too big so sent pants and girls' vests. Went down to Clayesmore [Preparatory] School [in Charlton Marshall] – J.R. thinks John had better go there. They have an excellent woman there working up a pre-prep class. The headmaster seems a nice man. I am not very good at asking the sort of things parents ought to know but we went all over and it seems infinitely preferable to the Grammar School with their appalling buildings. Delivered notes for John's party next week.

Friday, January 9. John and I went to Bournemouth to get presents for his party and a pair of shoes for me. I did not have to pay more for them than two years ago – £2 – but a skirt was 4 guineas so I might as well have made one. We had a horrid lunch, soup and a very peppery tomato and egg dish and awful fruit jelly, just gelatine and cochineal. Went to the newsreel theatre to see Mickey Mouse. The place was full of children and the boy in front gave John a piece of chocolate.

Saturday, January 10. A lot of typing at the WVS and hospital work.

Sunday, January 11. Made a toboggan with John's new tools. It won't hold together but perhaps we shall have no snow.

Monday, January 12. Sent more clothes for the [Tarrant] Hinton boy. The girl's vest won't do and he wants bigger knickers and a second jersey. Gay has come back. She took the children for a lovely holiday to her sister and had no chores to do and there was a girl who took out all the children and now she feels a new woman. She is going to fix up Richard at Clayesmore.

Wednesday, January 14. Went to Bournemouth to buy cakes for the party. Bought a skirt and cardigan at a less frequented shop at normal prices – 30s and 18s 9d. The shop only heated by electric heaters and the assistants old and cold. Had a lovely lunch because we went earlier – good soup, teal[3] casserole and a jam puff. John had soup with vegetables and cheese and biscuits.[4]

Thursday, January 15. There is a new scheme for the WVS to darn all the troops' socks. They are to arrive washed and those too bad to mend are to be put on one side and will be sent to contractors to re-foot, and the Army will find the darning wool.

---

[3] A teal is a type of duck.

[4] Food and nutrition were persistent concerns. In her Directive Response for Mass-Observation this month, Phyllis reported that 'All the members of my family have lost weight – my husband a stone, my Mother three stones and both my Father and myself a half stone. We have had no "flu" last winter or this so far and are very well, throwing off colds quickly. We are very hungry. My husband looks and feels better than he has for years but this may be due to an interesting job rather than a better diet.' (Directive Response, January 1942.)

Circularised the villages to know how many they would darn. This village is already involved with the local Camp but so far the difficulty has been wool as the thin stuff is no good for hand knitted socks. Mother has got her coupon free voucher and bought some with that.

Friday, January 16. John's party. A great success but a bit rowdy and I felt at the end that the little ones had not had quite a fair deal. One of his friends had just started at the Grammar School and had lurid tales to tell so that we were glad that we had decided on Clayesmore. The whole show was nearly wrecked by John's loose tooth coming nearly out an hour before they came. He was so frightened but with a looking glass he was calm by the time and lost it completely by tea time. They all liked their hidden presents and I managed to get a cake with chocolate icing and we had crackers and chocolate biscuits and jelly. Kathleen gave us the milk.

Saturday, January 17. Tea with the Killicks. Mrs. Johnson asked for a layette, another one from Charles Street. They pass on the good news from one to the next. She is a welfare mother [*i.e., receiving welfare payments*] and really tries and lives to a system and has her hair brushed first thing in the morning. She is only on the borderline of deserving because her husband has a rations allowance of £1 which keeps up her income well over 30s a week. A Mrs. Berry also applied but she has five children and is having a sixth and seems to be planning to go back to London and really does not want to take them back shabby. She did not want to see the Assistance Board but had gone to Mr. H. who obviously had not committed himself. She had made friends with Mrs. Tracy who brought John Smith round the other day and had heard that I might be induced to yield something. I rashly gave Mrs. Tracy some second-hand things for illegitimate babe, thinking it was hard for her to see the other child being fitted up with new. She is the worst type of Irish Catholic and has no regard for the truth. I told Mrs. Berry I would ask Mr. H. and let her know. J.R. had planned to come this weekend but he rang up with an awful cold and put it off. Mrs. Berry sent her children round with almost bare feet to know if she could have the clothes. I found Mr. H. thought they were quite unworthy and should spend their rail fares on clothing. I had no decent second-hand clothes for so many so sent her a note to go to the Soldiers', Sailors' and Airmen's Families Association person as she is a soldier's wife and they have a lot of clothes.

Tuesday, January 20. Very frozen everywhere. The Stuarts went to Bath but I went up [to their house at Letton] and sorted all the clothes from the Blandford working party and marked some of them with the sizes in the neck. I am pleased that my care in sending out each garment with directions has meant that only three things came back wrong and they were quite easily put right. The knitting isn't so good – all the scarves are too short. Went down to see Mrs. T. in the afternoon and took her Father's magic cure for lumbago. Met the Killicks on their way to us with waste paper so John returned with them and I picked him up on my return.

Wednesday, January 21. John went to the new school. I think it will work alright. I get down at 7 and make one bed before I do the downstairs rooms. Then I fly up from breakfast and make the rest and we start at 8.30, John on the back of my bicycle wrapped up in two pairs of gloves, balaclava, scarf, coat and mackintosh. We got there at '9' and I was back again here by 9 [*sic*] and do the bedroom and still get up to Mrs. Stuart soon after 10. I have to leave at 10 to 12 but soon I shall be able to leave John to come all the way home alone. He was a bit tearful on being left as it was so dark[5] and there were so many big boys but when I fetched him he was very happy. Richard, who was quite happy at the start, was very white and insisted on coming back with me and John rather than have a lift in the car with the others. They were both dead tired all the afternoon.

Thursday, January 22. John's birthday. I am glad we had the party before – he would have been too tired to enjoy it today. We kept his parcels until after school. It is such a mistake to have Christmas and birthday so close. Sorted and packed Red Cross things at WVS and made room for more. Mrs. Stuart does waste so much time just doodling round instead of getting on with the job in hand. She has so many irons in the fire that it takes so long to bring her mind to bear on the matter in hand.

Friday, January 23. Sent out more needlework and typed directions. Had tea at the Killicks. The children had a picnic by themselves and we had a nice gossip in the other room.

Saturday, January 24. Mrs. Tracy has tried to interest me in another customer, her landlady's daughter – in fact, the whole household and herself. The child had such bad chilblains and no shoes, and they had been sent to Mr. H. I let her try on the second-hand shoes but none would fit so they are seeing the Assistance Board. I said I would see them again when they had a form from him.

Sunday, January 25. Took John to Sunday school. Richard came back with us and played until 12.30 when we saw [*word missing*] on the right side of the road home.

Monday, January 26. Work from Milton Abbas came back to the depot all wrong. They hold working parties at three different houses and the maids give extra wool if people come at odd times, and they have made helmets of the scarf wool and wrong patterns. They are very nice and think they can avoid it next time. The coupons for John Smith's extensive wardrobe have turned up from his mother, to my great relief. John was sent home from school with a cough. They had such an epidemic of whooping cough last term I suppose their nerve is bad, but it was only going into the warm after the cold ride. What I should do if I was working in a munition factory I cannot think, with no one much to leave him with.

Tuesday, January 27. The coupons for the [Tarrant] Hinton boy have come in now so I shall be alright for my returns at the end of the month. They sent me a vast quantity of under 5's shoes for the clothing depot.

Wednesday, January 28. Mother's darning party for the Down House camp seems to have come to an end. There were no socks this week and she has never had the amount she undertook. Cooperation seems very difficult. You get your part going and everyone keen for nothing.

---

[5] Daylight saving measures (moving the clocks forward) led to dark winter mornings. See Glossary.

Thursday, January 29. Mrs. Stuart's dying aunt is very low with a cough. The doctor's coming rather interrupts work as I have to retire while they discuss her condition. I typed out directions for the hospital regarding casualties, where the overflow are to be sent and where to get transport. They have abandoned the idea of turning the cinema into a hospital within the tank island, for which matron is very thankful. Ruth [Grundy] came to tea to tell us how she is getting on in her resident day nursery. The matron still would have preferred an extra nurse so she does not encourage the teaching and Ruth finds it difficult to make much progress. They still do not respond to stories but are quick at picking up games and wildly excited with scissors for cutting out, brushes and paint. She seems to be put on a great deal but that would be her own fault, I have no doubt. The Mayoress had a jumble sale for the District Hospital Supply Service and made £50 with junk, mostly bought up by evacuees, so they said, but as their houses have the barest minimum of furniture they would be able to find a use for most stuff. Lady Bruce-Gardner called to inspect some of the working parties the same afternoon and the wonderful result was made known, so it was very nice for Mrs. B., and her working party has made 100 garments since December. Father went to a lecture for the Home Guard and others on the strategy of defending towns such as this and why we expect invasion.[6] He came back very interested and they had all sat there spellbound for two hours and no one had fidgeted.

21. Blandford Home Guard

Friday, January 30. Drew up rough draft of the District Supply Service report for the local paper. We have done very much less work this year.

Sunday, February 1. An Australian sergeant pilot turned up. He knew relations of my Mother out there and in Canada. He was a charming person and interested in and about everything. He did not seem to be so anti-British as I expected. He told us that

[6] A few weeks later Phyllis wrote 'I expect invasion. I am very much afraid of how I shall behave when it comes but I feel prepared mentally and we all have our jobs to do here in the village if it comes so I cannot do any more about it. I wish we had more Molotov cocktails to throw at the tanks if they come up the road but I have looked at a Tommy gun and know how to load and fire it so I could do something if it came to it.' (Directive Response, March 1942.) As a public notice from August 1942 indicates, fears of invasion persisted for much of this year – see p. 132.

Victoria province[7] was considered very early Victorian by New South Wales, which confirms my sister's impressions, but he also said that industry over there was all out for war production while she said you would hardly know there was a war. He seems to enjoy his leave and going about town but is very apt to judge our war prices with their own pre-war and they expect to have shoes made and sports jackets and to buy Burberrys, which seems hardly fair on the civilian population which has to clothe itself.

Monday, February 2. Headquarters at Dorchester wrote about a new scheme they want to try out in rural areas to distribute meat pies to the villagers. The General was all against it but if it could be run in with school meals from the British Restaurant it would be quite easy.

Tuesday, February 3. A Mrs. H. wanted a wool permit. I could not think why it was suggested that I should call in on my way home and stamp her card then and there. However, it turned out her husband was the only coal man who would haul from the station for the house. Had tea with the Killicks. Gay is giving a demonstration of slipper making at a village Women's Institute meeting. She is good at it.

Wednesday, February 4. The ATS at the Camp applied to us for some clothes for a girl who was being discharged after conviction for a civil offence. She would be allowed to keep her underclothes and a pair of shoes but nothing else and as she was an orphan and destitute when she joined they were at their wits' end to clothe her. I fitted her up very easily from secondhand things. Infant Welfare day but so cold that not many babies came.

Monday, February 9. Our precious Rachel has developed a pain in her chest and been most depressed, imagining she had awful diseases. She went to the doctor who said she needed to rest and must only do light work and if the medicine he gave her did no good she would have to knock off for a bit. We rush round waiting on her and carrying trays and now she remembers that in her rush in the morning she rode into a dustbin and fell onto the handle of the old lid, which must have been what gave her the pain.

Tuesday, February 10. Mrs. Stuart says there is a scheme to take over the old food office and make the ground floor into a nicer British Restaurant and keep the present one for school dinners only and to use the rest of the building for a hostel for the ATS who have nowhere away from the Camp.[8]

Wednesday, February 11. Went down to the Killicks. The vet came to break the ice on the horse trough and talked about his horses. He shot ten at the beginning of the

---

[7] She is confused here. Administrative divisions in Australia are called states.

[8] Changes were to occur that summer. 'After serving some thousands of meals at the parish-room, the British Restaurant was moved on Tuesday to new premises in West Street and its place at the parish-room was taken by a new canteen purely for elementary school children, which started serving meals on Wednesday. The British Restaurant will not reopen immediately. The County Council has refunded expenditure by the [Blandford] Corporation on the parish-room.' (*Western Gazette*, Friday, July 3rd, 1942 p. 2.)

war and is trying to keep the well bred colts and a few mares until it is over. He has ploughed up two minute fields to grow oats so the neighbours will have to keep their chickens in when they are sown.

Thursday, February 12. The Stuarts went off to Bath to have his teeth out. Mrs. C. arrived on the doorstep to ask for help again! I gave her secondhand stuff in September and the Assistance Board interviewed her and the Soldiers', Sailors' and Airmen's Families Association loaded her with gifts – and now could I get her a pram, as hers was broken, and some clothes for the baby she is going to have? She was just as dirty and miserable as ever she was. I think she must have sold the other things. I have never seen her seeing better days.

Saturday, February 14. Ran into Mrs. T., the first evacuee I ever visited. In the course of conversation she told me Mrs. C. had said she was coming to me for help but Mrs. T. did hope I would not [help] because she was much better off than others. Her husband lived out and she had £1 a week to feed him on and she did not give any of it back to him for what he had to spend at the Camp and she was always borrowing money and went to the pictures with it and her house was filthy. I was glad that I had been firm. Mrs. T. approves of points rationing and says she gets a lot more things now than she did. Soap did not worry her but she is so clean and has three [children] under five that I should have thought the situation would have been desperate. Happily we have a lot of toilet soap in hand so we shall be able to get through. Warships Week began.[9] We took out the young to see the procession but the crowd was not so dense as last time. The boys did not want to see it on its way back because they were so afraid of not seeing the anti-aircraft gun in the marketplace, so we hung about in the bitter wind and got them places in the very front. But the co-operation planes did not turn up so it was not very exciting.[10] The squad of ATS were very well thought of and several girls thought it would not be so bad if they were made to go in them in the end. Ethel, who went to the milk factory, thought now she has to work so hard that the ATS might have been preferable.

Monday, February 16. This awful cold goes on and on. It is all I can do to make myself go up to Letton. Happily there is nothing much to do and no typing.

Thursday, February 19. I helped at the baby show for Warships Week. The prizes were savings stamps. The entries were poor compared with War Weapons Week, but that was summer. I helped at the door taking particulars. It was interesting seeing how a baby show is run. Three trained nurses were the judges and they agreed very well. I do not think it was advertised enough.

Saturday, February 21. They did not make the target, £155,000, but they closed at £75,500, which is more than the hull of a corvette but not much towards its equipment.

---

[9] Organized by the National War Savings Committee, Warships Weeks encouraged people to donate towards the cost of building a specific ship.

[10] It had previously been announced that on this day, for Warship Week, 'Admiral G.T.C.P. Swaby is to open Blandford's campaign which is intended to raise enough money to float a corvette. There will be the largest procession Blandford has ever seen, with at least five bands.' (*Western Gazette*, 30 January 1942, p. 3.)

The real savings in the villages did well. I was amazed at our £161 but the school mistress says the money is all there in the family pockets if only you can fetch it out.[11]

Sunday, February 22. Mother's little old nurse of 97 is breaking up.[12] She fell out of bed and has been brought downstairs to a bed in her sitting room and I must listen for her in the night.

Monday, February 23. She will have to have someone to sit with her all night. She can't help herself and I went in several times. Our evacuee has done the job many times and has taken it on. She can even lay out how we have been rewarded for taking her in although she spoilt John even worse than I knew she would.

Tuesday, February 24. Seabrook seems to be sinking. We all think about her rations, which she has not been eating for some time, living on bread and milk and vegetables and gravy.[13]

Food, of course, was a crucial concern to everyone, and Phyllis replied to Mass-Observation's February Directive that enquired about provisions in the following way.

The food situation seems easier round here and the points system is popular. People say they have a chance for things they never thought it worth asking for before, like tinned fruit and dried fruit. The severe milk rationing has only just begun to operate but now we find the powdered milk is alright we are not so overcome. Fish was very bad last month but now it is plentiful and very nice. Some weeks there seems to be nothing – no rabbits or suet or liver at the butcher's and no fish – and the next week you can have everything you ask for. I think most people's attitude is that we expect it and we are luckier than most, which is what I heard two gypsy women saying in the baker's and you would not expect them to know much that is going on abroad. Everyone agrees that you must shop early to get what you want and that shops are not impartial. The ones that will let anyone have what they ask for are very well thought of and the ones which have a special drawer for Mrs. X's bacon are shunned, but we are all glad when our own tradesmen tell us of something nice they have or are holding for us. *(Directive Response, February 1942.)*

[11] These financial estimates were sometimes not entirely reliable. The *Western Gazette* for 12 February, p. 12, claimed that the goal of this campaign was £120,000, whereas two weeks later (26 February, p. 5) it judged the campaign successful since around £75,000 had been raised and the corvette would cost £55,000.

[12] Earlier she had given Maria Seabrook's age as 93. Seabrook must have been one of the few inhabitants of wartime Blandford who had been born in the 1840s.

[13] The implication is that, if and when Seabrook died, the household will lose rations that she, for the most part, did not consume.

There was no entry in Phyllis's diary for Wednesday, February 25 because this was the day that M-O's volunteers – here acting as 'Directive Respondents' – were asked to describe in the form of a 'day survey'. She wrote the following.

6.30. Made cup of tea for myself and evacuee who is attending as night nurse to my Mother's old nurse of 97 who is dying at last. Got back into bed and read to John until 7. Got up and made three beds and dusted two rooms and undid blackout. Got John up for 8 o'clock breakfast.
8.30 Cleared away breakfast. Took John to school two miles away on the back of my bicycle.
9.15. Returned and did the bedroom. As it was not my day for the WVS, I took my Mother's place with the invalid and knitted in there until 12 when I brought my own [child] and other children home. I only do this on Wednesdays. Other days I ride home quickly with John on the back.
1.00. Lunch, after which I cleared away and then had rest with John, reading and knitting.
3.00. Went down to the Killicks to borrow typewriter.[14] John played with Richard and Judy while I talked to Mrs. Killick and Mrs. W., who works for her one day a week when she has canteen and British Restaurant.
4.15. Returned and fed chickens and filled up [coal] scuttles as the gardener has a bad cold and only comes for a bit in the morning.
4.30. Made the tea and took up my Mother's. Made toast for the rest of us.
5.00. Did some odd writing jobs. Shut up the chickens and stoked boilers in garage and greenhouse.
6.00. Gave John his supper and put him to bed.
7.15. Went down to the sitting room and had a good warm up and read the papers.
8.00. Supper. Cleared away and washed up as Rachel went away early to a dance. Listened to the newscast at 9, dozed and read and knitted until 10 and went to bed.[15]

Thursday, February 26. Seabrook better and stronger but hardly eating anything. She is not cross any more but very sleepy and contented.

Monday, March 2. My cousin Ruth rang me up at the WVS about the ATS in the town. She is the Commandant and has a welfare fund from which she has to provide comforts for them all over the place. She wants the WVS to take care of the odd ones who are working at messes in the town. One lot wants curtains for their sitting room and another lot have got a settee which needs a cover. I said we would take them on and told Mrs. Stuart, who is asking two friends of hers who have daughters in the Services to see to it for her. Unpacked needlework from working parties. One lot of knitting is wrong again – scarves made from different kinds of wool and special wool knitted up into anything. I explained most carefully to them last time, so as I cannot be rude I shall have to undo it all and send it out again. We do not get much bad work

[14] Phyllis borrowed a typewriter in the winter and in the summer used her Father's in the brewery office. (Directive Response, March 1942.)

[15] A few months later, when asked about her 'belief in the news', she said 'I believe the facts are true as far as they go and put a far more pessimistic interpretation upon them than either the BBC or the newspaper', though she thought that the BBC had become more realistic in its reporting and was not just giving pep talk. (Directive Response, June 1942.)

on the whole. The village Rest Centre is to be inspected so went round to several people to ask them to come and see my Mother while she is sitting with our invalid and have their parts assigned to them. Met Mrs. M.[16] who was on her way into the town to order a table shelter. Her daughter is now with them for the duration, and they had one up in the North and were so comfortable under it. He is the head maltster in the brewery so they feel if the building comes down on top of them they will be alright. Mother and Father went out to a dinner party at the hotel. This was an event – her goddaughter is being married tomorrow and this was to meet the relations. Mother had her clothes taken in for the occasion and was so afraid she would be cold and everyone else would have beautiful hands.

Tuesday, March 3. They thoroughly enjoyed themselves last night. The dinner was very good vegetable soup, a mess of fish with a piquant sauce over it, pheasant, and hock cup to drink. Mother most distressed that the hostess carried off the ladies before she had finished hers, and Father said it was all he could do not to finish off the lady's next to him when she had gone. All Mother's fears were groundless. She was beautifully warm and the bridegroom's mother had hands as bad as hers and was living just the same life and they had a lovely time comparing notes.[17] I had a letter from the County Commissioner for the Girl Guides asking me to restart the Ranger Company in the town to fit in with the new registering of 16 year olds. If only they had asked me a year ago I should have taken it on. I ran a company in the village years ago when we were so terribly keen and straight from school but it would be uphill work now. I took care of the invalid while Mother went to the wedding. If only I had known she would hang on like this I would have refused my invitation and saved 10s in a wedding present.

Wednesday, March 4. The Rest Centre inspection took place. All was in order and the personnel assembled at the right time. The desks have all to be piled up in the yard. Mrs. Stuart was most efficient and helpful about it and it is to be open when the Home Guard have their big manoeuvres at the weekend.

Thursday, March 5. Infant Welfare in the afternoon. Quite a lot of babies and toddlers being immunised for diphtheria. Terrible screams from one but only because her bricks had to be taken away to get her arm out of her sleeve. Ruth Grundy came in to tell us she was giving up her job at the resident day nursery because she could not manage the long hours. Since one child was burnt there has to be one person with the children all the time, which seems to [be] her, even having her meals brought in on a tray. The place seems to be very badly run and I said if she really thought so badly of it she had no right to leave on account of ill health and not report the real reasons

---

[16] Mrs Mantell, wife of Jim Mantell, a long-serving employee at the Brewery (information from Julian Walther.)

[17] Ladies faced challenges because of the departure from large houses of domestic servants, who were volunteering or being called up for national service. Hand care had become a problem for many women, particularly those doing unaccustomed domestic chores. In the Directive Response for January, Phyllis had reported, 'I cannot get glycerine, which I use for my hands in cold weather. I am using an old pot of zinc and castor oil which I found I had put away. I have heard of two cases of people adversely affected by the disappearance of liquid paraffin.'

22. Blandford Rest Centre armband

why she felt she could not stay. She said that matron used a ruler on the children and shut them up in cupboards when they were naughty.

Friday, March 6. Went to Dorchester by bus to a meeting of clothing organisers. I had plenty of time to spare so looked at the shops first. Found a biscuit queue in Marks and Spencer so got a pound and some sweets, which was very lucky. There was plenty of dried milk too, which we cannot get. The meeting was good and helpful. I did not know that Southampton children now got their clothes with the same form as the London ones and through the school teacher. I must be very strong-minded with the [village] representatives, I see. Apart from two pair of shoes I have given out, I have no guilty conscience. The welfare officers were there and they will do any interviewing and be helpful in the villages with difficult cases. Quite a lot of people find that the Assistance Board either hands the cases for investigation back to them or else are too lenient and do not ask enough questions, but as the welfare officer said, they are understaffed and many of their best interviewers have been called up. I had a nice lunch afterwards – roast beef and Yorkshire pudding and greens followed by date pudding and coffee – but it took so long that I had very little time afterwards and had to catch the bus home.

Saturday, March 7. The Home Guard exercises began at 2 in the afternoon. Gay was registering and left the children here to play but she did not see any excitements. The dive bombers began at 6.30 and they came right over the house and dropped a smoke bomb on the brewery – it was meant to represent a high explosive. Father was on duty from 6 to 8 and from 12 to 2 at night and then 6 to 8 in the morning. There were sentries on the bridge and we hoped that the opposing forces would attack our end and we should see the fun. Rachel came back in the evening quite easily – there were plenty of bombs about. We heard that bombs had really been dropped on my sister's old farm at Delcombe. One huge crater in a field. The cows might have been there but no damage done and the rest in the woods.

Sunday, March 8. Not much excitement in the night and Rachel got here alright but had to show her identity card to get through. I remembered to feed the chickens and do the stoves as R.[18] is a sergeant and in charge of three pill boxes. He turned up about 7 looking dead to the world but had had a happy time. They had wiped out the attackers at their end but the referee had allowed one attack again and before he had got his pill boxes reorganised they had had some success. They had caught a spy getting through. The main trouble was the troops already in the town for the pictures. They were told to arrest anyone in a forage cap but it was impossible to do it with the numbers already in, so that saboteurs wrecked the post office and he thought the railway. They would have liked more ammunition because they only had fire crackers and they lasted no time while the attacked[19] had plenty of blank. The older men were dead tired by the morning as there were not enough of them to rest at all and Rideout was on his feet all the time going from his headquarters to his pill boxes. They had 15 regulars from the Camp recruits doing Heavy Artillery training and they had not much idea of an ordinary rifle but they all had a good time together.

23. One of the many 'pill-boxes' that were built to defend Blandford from invasion

[18] It is probable that Phyllis is here referring to Rideout, the family's gardener, chauffeur, and general handyman.

[19] She probably meant 'the attackers' here.

Monday, March 9. Undid parcels of work at the WVS. The same village in trouble again, wanting khaki wool for scarves when I have just sent them some RAF.[20] They had not read the letter I sent them with it and would have made it all up into gloves so it is just as well they rang up. The children in the school have subscribed a pound and want to buy wool for the working party to knit up into comforts for their school mates who are now in the RAF. This gives us quite a problem because Red Cross materials cannot be used for particular individuals. I think the girls will have to get coupon free wool on their clothing cards and each give the name of one boy. Father came in and said that he had seen Major C., the head of the Home Guard here, and he was quite satisfied with the practice from their point of view. Mrs. Stuart got in a muddle with one of her Rest Centres because they had not told her that it was to be a hospital for the night and the Red Cross detachment were to get it ready as such, so she turned them all out. I had a post card from my husband at last – the first word since the end of January. He has been travelling about and very cold.

Tuesday, March 10. The Stuarts went to Salisbury to have the rest of his teeth out but I went up to the house and packed up scarves and balaclavas. It is difficult now one has to weigh all the garments and get these weights to agree with the wool as sent. They are having warfare up there in the household about the soap ration. Mrs. Stuart thought she would leave things for a week after the ration came in, not realising how tight it was, and by the end everybody was accusing everybody else of using up the soap, so now she has a ration scheme of her own but with two nurses and so many old servants it isn't easy and as she says it will mean that they have none for themselves. Left early and went round the town buying buttons and girdles for the needlework. The shops are so short of buttons that they won't even let the Central Hospital Supply Service have anything like what we want and we don't seem able to get them from the Personal Service League. Ruth Grundy came in again and she had met a nice person on the Committee who had said that she hoped they would be able to reach agreement with her at the day nursery, so now she thinks that she will stay on if she can have her weekends. Of course what she is missing is the long school holidays she has had to recuperate in all her life. She has looked round Blandford without seeing a chance of an easier job and none of the schools need a kindergarten teacher. We had a letter from Australia written just after Christmas. She says all plans for evacuating the schools to the interior are complete and she knows just what she has to do. They had a very exhausting Christmas – very unlike India. No maid, cold chicken instead of turkey, but Christmas pudding and no end of washing up, and the hottest day you can think of, everybody quite wilted by it except the small boy with a new motorcar.

Wednesday, March 11. Went up to the surgery to see Dr. Wilson who says I am having a baby in September. I shall feel I am doing something for the war effort at last because I can still do the clothing depot and keep an eye on the needlework and with no one to take care of John I cannot go off and run a hostel for munition workers, which is what I really could do. I never wanted an only child but I had to wait two

---

[20] The RAF wore blue.

years until I was free of relatives after being trepanned,[21] and then coming down here, expecting anything to happen, it did not seem fair to land the family with an infant in arms, but it's now or never so I am very glad. He was very interesting about the Home Guard exercise from the control room end. They had a gas bomb outside and did not shut the window so that they were nearly overcome before they got their masks on. The head man cannot get his glasses on inside so could not read the messages. The referee cut two of their telephone lines and fused their lights early on but they recovered very well from that. On the Sunday Mr. Hall,[22] the head and the rector, said he would not be there so Mr. S. deputised for him and had a casualty label put on him first thing on Sunday morning, which left hardly anyone there, but he seems to have managed. There will be postmortems soon. I was afraid he [the doctor] might be having his holiday in September but he says he cannot take one for certain but all the same they work harder than munition workers or miners and they must have them.

My cousin Ruth came in about a dump of things for the ATS to be left here for the WVS. Apparently she went direct to Lady Stavordale as Mrs. Stuart has been difficult again. I wish it wasn't always my relations she feels are so impossible that she cannot bring herself to work with them. She did not tell Ruth anything about the proposed scheme for taking on the old food office and turning the ground floor into a new British Restaurant and the first into a hostel for the ATS. Ruth heard rumours of it and gave Mrs. Stuart every opportunity to tell her of it but she didn't so she thought it was only just rumour but the Mayor swore to her that it was true. Meanwhile the Government decided to take over another building as a club room and Ruth got a promise of help from WVS headquarters to help with the furnishing so she rang up Mrs. P., who she heard had had a lot of second-hand furniture put on one side for her for the food office hostel, and when she asked her about it she dithered and said she thought the whole scheme was in abeyance. I dare say it was the Education people who hesitated over taking over the present British Restaurant for the school children that has made Mrs. Stuart keep quiet, and she would not know how gossip gets round, but when people don't like it, it just makes things worse and worse. I rang her up on Tuesday evening and she had just been up to the Camp to see the ATS people up there and came back so charmed with them that she was ready to do anything for them, and brought away 10 lbs of wool to be knitted up into comforts in three weeks but hardly a mention of Ruth and no thought of working in with her. It is so stupid and such a waste of time and energy. If only she had had to work in the last war and had learnt to get on with women we should be saved all this silly nonsense. I am a rotten secretary. I ought to have her feeding out of my hand by now and be able to prevent these major blunders.

Thursday, March 12. Called in at the mess to measure the window for the curtains. They seemed nice girls and had a roaring great fire blazing in their sitting room, which looked very nice. Mother thinks we have a pair she has lent as blackout every

---

[21] Phyllis had undergone surgery for a brain tumour sometime in the later 1930s. Writing a few weeks later about death, she disclosed that 'I did nearly die a few years ago and thought about it quite a lot then but now I feel that is all behind me and when it comes it comes'. (Directive Response, May 1942).

[22] Revd. Charles Frank Hall, OBE, rector of Blandford Forum since 1935 (Kelly's *Post Office Directory*, 1939.)

now and then which will do. Typed out knitting directions for the ATS comforts. No one is very enthusiastic about knitting for girls who ought to be able to do it for themselves.

Friday, March 13. Miss B.[23] called me aside at the school to say that one of the Day boys is away with mumps but we will not tell the children. The contact seems rather remote so perhaps they will not get it. I arranged all the ATS wool and despatched it. It was done up in 12 ounce hank with 4 ounces in each skein which makes it difficult to sort. The Killick family came to tea and had a happy time. Our old invalid is past being upset by the noise but she hangs on.

Saturday, March 14. A day at home. Housework and shopping in the morning. Fetched the joint and the fish. We are having pork this week – what a treat. Did some greenhouse gardening in the afternoon and went down to the Killicks for tea. Sawed up wood for her and the boys got at the woodpile while we were talking and heaved the biggest logs all over the place.

Sunday, March 15. My busy day. Washed up and took John to Sunday school, came home after a slight gossip with Gay to do the washing and cook the dinner. The pork was done – a treat – only I had no cornflour to thicken the gravy, but we had bottled windfalls for apple sauce so everything was alright. Dug over John's garden in the afternoon where he is going to have vegetables, after which we went for a short bicycle ride. I don't regret the expense of the bicycle as he now rides very confidently and I could not have gone on riding down with him on my carrier. Wrote letters after tea and helped with a Meccano model until bedtime, when I got all the ironing done before supper. Rachel has asked to have every Sunday evening off in future instead of alternate mornings and evenings, which will make Sunday an easier day.

Monday, March 16. Mrs. Stuart had a visit from the Army blood transfusion service, who are going to have a new drive next week to get more donors. The General was very irate about it and especially about the team having to be billeted locally for the inside of the week. They had had no success in getting billets so far but they won't as long as they ring up their own friends who are completely devastated by losing servants. If they approach people who only kept one maid they would be much luckier because they are used to their visitors giving a hand. Planted a few flower seeds in pots in the greenhouse for John, with his help. There is not much room with trays of onions at every turn and peas and cabbages waiting for the spring. Made some bee syrup and started slow stimulation in the hives. I hope we have a better season this year. Rita came in. She is Commandant of the Red Cross and had trouble with Mrs. Stuart over the girls' school at the Home Guard exercise. They are in the middle of postmortems. On the night they had quite a lot of real casualties when they only expected make believe ones. A lorry load of ATS were overturned, and a man with malaria and another with a rigor leading to pneumonia. She is still living alone with an occasional maid and finds she is getting more and more picniky. She is having a water heater put into her hot water tank to simplify the hot water question.

---

[23] John Walther remembers his teacher as Miss Bennett.

Wednesday, March 18. Had a day at home. The van came over from Dorchester in the afternoon with a variety of clothing for distribution to the Rest Centres. It is to be kept in three dumps in private houses, one in Blandford itself, one on the Dorchester side, and the other on the Wimborne side. There seem plenty of clothes but as usual nothing for the not-so-slim. Father came in at lunch saying they had had great complaints of Mr. H., the head of the ARP, during the Home Guard exercises. He treated the rural people very badly and gave them no room to do their part and insisted on all telephone calls going through his hands.

Thursday, March 19. Mrs. Stuart came down and had a look at the clothing and is going to contact the people and get it dispersed. Met Ruth in the town. She was taken ill at the nursery school and brought home and the doctor has told her she cannot go back so that seems to be the end. She had gone back and collected her things and said goodbye, but having had a row with the member of the committee who secured her services, she is now thinking of writing to the committee criticising the way the place is run. I cannot think why it is so bad when she says inspectors come in and out very often. We heard from a cousin of my Mother's, and that nurse that went mad on my sister is working in a splendid nursery school in Weston. All the staff are trained nurses and she is the only one with nursery experience and is in charge of 30 under two. She quite recovered after being certified and they feel it was all a bad dream. She just has to live with women and not married couples. Kathleen and Peter came over to tea. Peter very amused at a meeting they had had of the Portman Hunt and all the farmers had wanted to keep it going. He said if they were working as hard as they should be they would not have the time. One farmer who used to live only for the horses once was keenest about putting the hounds down until the end of the war, but the younger ones would not have it and they put the matter back.[24] Kathleen's nurse is not even going to be interviewed. Kathleen only said that she was a farmer's wife and that the children had to have their first lessons at home because there are no older children living in their valley who could take them to the village school. She said nothing about having all the garden to do – so they are all very relieved.

Friday, March 20. Mrs. Cuff met me at the ATS sitting room in C____ mess and we cut out the cover for the settee. It is an awful shape and the stuff (brown blackout) is horrible to work. The girls were not interested at all but polite. We felt they were quite happy with it as it was and we were wasting our far more valuable time. The floor had been scrubbed and was very wet and the covers on the other chairs were damp all round the bottom but they are going to have linoleum in time. We both agreed that we would never have let our houses furnished to the Army as this one has been.

---

[24] 'Blandford Town Hall was crowded on Wednesday afternoon [April 15] at the adjourned annual meeting of the Portman Hunt – held to decide whether hunting should be continued next season. When the meeting opened a month ago a recommendation by the Hunt Committee that hunting should cease for the duration of the war, and a nucleus of the pack be retained at the kennels – which Captain the Hon. Gerald Portman had intimated could still be used during the war – was not carried; and the meeting adjourned in order that landowners, farmers and subscribers should be given the opportunity of attending.' The verdict was for the hunt to be continued but not for more than two days per week. (*Bournemouth Daily Echo*, 16 April 1942, p. 2.)

Monday, March 23. We have been asked to organise Buttercup Day again.[25] Mrs. Stuart hates flag days but the old General loves counting all the money and never making a mistake, although he grumbles all the time. The appeal is very well done and they are willing to send all the tins and flowers direct from London so there is nothing to do except tell people they are coming and to collect some collectors. Gave out a lot of needlework and called in some stray garments which have been out in some villages for months. We want to send off some of the completed orders and make room for what is out now.

Tuesday, March 24. More needlework came back. Typed notices for Buttercup Day. Machined the settee cover.

Wednesday, March 25. No WVS. Turned out the nursery and cleaned the windows. Fetched the children from school. John went to dinner at the Killicks and I met with Mrs. Cuff at 2 to fit the settee cover. The Major of the ATS came in while we were there and wanted us to do a great deal more to beautify the room but we said we had not time and it would be a waste when I am sure it does not matter in the least to the girls. Mrs. Cuff said afterwards that if they would lend her an O.T.[26] to take the place of her maid who has been called up she would do it but she is cooking for the same number single handed as the girls, of whom we see five.

Thursday, March 26. Father said that one of the blood transfusion propaganda team had been to visit the brewery and had enrolled a great number of volunteers, including himself. He had thought he was too old but she had said that people of 80 had given blood very satisfactorily.[27]

Friday, March 27. Issued vouchers for coupon free wool. Typed out directions for making men's pants. We thought it would a nice change for everyone but seeing what a fuss there has been over the boys' shirts I have doubts now, especially now I hear that Mrs. Blandford's people are losing their initial keenness. Mrs. Cuff complained of the pattern but that is my fault because I wanted them to look decent and not like mission garments so I gave up a good pattern I had for John but she says the cuff is unnecessarily complicated. I found by looking at a man's it was quite easy to do and a blessed relief after just acres of machining in pyjamas. She is a very skilled, good needlewoman so what she says goes. So I think I will collect up the rest of the shirts and do them myself. The pants seem simple enough. Mrs. Thorpe has approached the WVS about getting assistance over getting her cot and high chair down from London. I looked up the literature about it and it depends on the local authority, who can help if it thinks fit, so she must go to Mr. H. Went to tea with the Killicks.

---

[25] In the spring of 1941 a Buttercup Day had been organised in aid of the Orthopaedic Hospital for Crippled Children. (WRVS Archive, Monthly Narrative Report, Blandford Forum, May-June 1941.)

[26] This may mean 'other trade'. Dorothy Sheridan kindly advised us on this matter.

[27] It was later reported that 'Blandford and adjoining villages gave 333 volunteers in their three days' drive (Thursday, Friday, and Saturday) for the Army Blood Transfusion Service. . . The WVS organiser, Mrs. B.F.B. Stuart, organised an itinerary for the enrolment vans to visit all the villages in turn . . . and the local cinemas drew attention to the urgent need for volunteers.' (*Western Gazette*, 3 April 1942, p. 2.)

Saturday, March 28. No WVS. Did housework. Had my hair cut. Met Mrs. Cuff for a last fitting of the settee cover. Her daughters collect salvage in their neighbourhood on Saturdays, the very day when she would like a hand with the house. They take an enormous barrow they would never dream of using to help with the garden and have a most enjoyable time. Her husband gave me a glass of sherry one night and said as he poured it out 'I bet there isn't another bottle of that in this road', and they came back after their next collection and said 'You needn't think you're the only people to have a bottle of sherry. You should see the bottles Mrs. So-and-so puts out.' Went for a bicycle ride with John through the town, calling on Mrs. Thorpe on the way, but Mrs. Stuart had already been and said she would see to it for her, which is not what I should have done. I expect she was overcome at the sight of three children under five. Mrs. Thorpe had a whole lot to tell me about her relations having just been up to London to see them. Her father-in-law was marrying again and had sold her wireless set but she had stored her furniture in one room of a London County Council house and had given the key back to the office and they would see to it for her if she wanted to send for anything, and she only paid 4s 6d a week for it. It seemed plenty to me out of her Army allowance. She told me one disquieting thing – that the wool shop had allowed us to have light grey for the rest of coupon free wool and she had knitted some jumpers for the children so that means we must stop issuing vouchers for the whole 1½ lbs at once.[28]

Sunday, March 29. Sunday school with John, then the washing. Rachel stays at home every Sunday morning and has every Sunday afternoon and evening off instead and it makes much less of a rush with the work for me and is nicer for her. John went for a short ride with her in the afternoon and then we did a little harrowing in the field with a rake. Father let it to someone for a fortnight's grazing free, hoping the stock would pull out the rough grass as the brewery horses won't do it, but they don't seem to have done much good. I think it was too late in the season. My husband arrived in the evening on a motor bike, very tired and fed up with red tape. It's no wonder there are so many accidents at night. He said soldiers would step out into the road and try and get a lift. As he had a rucksack on he could not give a lift and he was so tired he might easily have ridden into someone as it was almost impossible to see them.

[28] The coupon-free wool was strictly for knitting garments for soldiers.

Monday, March 30. J.R. stayed in bed to breakfast, which kept him comfortable and out of the way of the housework. Did his washing after John went to school and we talked for the rest of the morning. Too cold to look at the bees so we had a bonfire of some old blackberry brambles, hoping they might bear better this year. Looked round the sheds and places to find somewhere to put some canaries which want breeding space. Found the very place but John and I must make it escape proof.

Tuesday, March 31. John broke up. He didn't seem to mind not having a prize even when Richard got the form prize. Miss Bennett seems to provide all the extras, like prizes, herself, which seems unnecessary. Ruth Grundy has been asked to go there next term as assistant to Miss Bennett. It will be a change after the nursery school. She is not going to take them for the three Rs but just for handiwork. She seems wildly enthusiastic, as she was about the other job. They [soldiers] were trying out a tank in the river which they had fitted up as an amphibian. It wasn't a great success as they could not land it and it seemed very difficult to handle in the water. They had been digging out the old ford all the morning, trying to get to a firm bottom, but all to no purpose. J.R. doubted the intelligence of the man handling it and it was a horrid pouring wet afternoon and in the end they hauled it out with a wire rope and dispersed. After watching that to the end we went over to see my sister at Melcombe. She had quite a party as an aged professor and his wife had taken rooms at the local pub to be near her and they came too and they all talked, but their minds are too academic for J.R. and his practical politics.[29] While we were out a batch of second-hand things came for the Rest Centres, among which were some women's coats I am glad to say.

Wednesday, April 1. J.R. gave me his traveller's ration book to collect up what I could for Mother. The butcher gave me two weeks' meat and four mutton chops for it which will be a lovely treat. He [J.R.] feeds so much in British Restaurants and says that he gets so tired of a cut off the joint and would love a shepherd's pie or rissole for a change. He went off at tea time looking a bit better and hopes to come down again soon.

Thursday, April 2. Sorted needlework at the WVS. Went to Mrs. B. and retrieved the five shirts she had left and she was glad to see the end of them. Went to Infant Welfare in the afternoon. Mrs. W. did not come so I weighed the infants, which was lovely and much nicer than standing up all the time sorting record sheets. They all seem to have put on weight so I am afraid my weighing must be a bit different but it might be just the spring. I know that lovely feeling when the baby has put on much more than you expected but I should hate the mothers to be disappointed next time.

Friday, April 3 [*Good Friday*].Went out with John on our bikes to get moss to decorate the font for Easter.

Saturday, April 4. Decorated the church. John played with Richard and Judy so I did not have to hurry. Had a nice chat to the rector's wife about her new officer's wife.

---

[29] Phyllis later portrayed her sister as a 'literary' person who liked to read (Directive Response, May 1942). Kathleen, writing under the name of Frances Woodhouse, was the author of a novel, *Country Holiday* (London: Allen & Unwin, 1935). Both J.R. and Phyllis leaned to the left politically.

Her husband is in the dental corps and never gets a sleeping out pass and has to feed in the mess always. She is much more homely than the last one and they have made the back kitchen into a separate kitchen so there is no friction at all. Went up to put the finished cover on the settee and John came too. He was disappointed that it was not more exciting in there.

Monday, April 6. Typed out a questionnaire to send to drivers for the WVS[30] to find out how many cars will go off the road in June and whether anyone would keep them on if they were given their licence and insurance and a maintenance allowance, or alternatively if they would lend their car to the WVS for the duration and would let other drivers use it.[31] We had an application for a wool permit from an aunt who wanted to knit for a nephew whose mother had already used up all her 1½ lbs for him but we had to refuse in the circumstances. Sowed John's seeds and collected stuffing for a scarecrow.

Tuesday, April 7. Finished off the scarecrow with clothes people had misguidedly sent for evacuees. It rained so hard last night that the seeds must have been washed out of the ground. Packed up gifts of garments for the County store. The brewery has a pub next door and will take the parcels for us but the lorry gets there much earlier than the storekeeper so they can only go on a fine day. Typed out thanks from the coal office for the help done by WVS members with coal cards. Had my hair cut, finished the ironing. Tied up carnations in the greenhouse.

Wednesday, April 8. John woke at 4. The gardener went off with flu but he has an old man to help him with the digging for a week or two so he may carry on. Turned out the nursery. Mrs. Stuart brought down the parcels for the County store. She was full of a scheme for making a film of the hospital and getting publicity for it. She wanted to see Father about it but he was out and about. John went to sleep all the afternoon so I got on with the boys' shirts.

Thursday, April 9. The people from the two rural Rest Centre dumps have been for their clothes so the room is a bit clearer. Mrs. Stuart forgot to ask Miss M. before school broke up so if there is an invasion in the holidays I shall never be able to get round to clothe anyone.

Friday, April 10. Rachel very anxious about her boy[friend] in the Middle East. His mother had a telegram to say he was on the danger list with wounds in the chest and thigh. One of our old maids was thinking of getting married but the boy is going to be court martialled. Apparently the last time he came down he was on duty as a despatch rider and came down on an Army bike. He has done it before and then he was fined £20 for the damage caused but he wasn't on duty then. His mother says he was always wild and did not mind if he was in work or not and as he is 25 it seems she picked a dud. Went to Kathleen's at Melcombe for the weekend. Her maid is going part-time on the land so Kathleen will probably only see her on wet days. She wants to go on living at home but she wants to have a uniform, to do which she must go away for a month's

[30] This was Easter Monday and a Bank Holiday. However, essential war-work carried on.

[31] No petrol would be allowed for personal travel after the end of June.

training and then they do not guarantee to send you home again. She should really go on the farm before she registers and then she would be left where she was but she is deaf and it is hard to make her understand. I slept out at my cousin's and her maid is being called up too. She doesn't mind about the uniform but wants to stay at home, but she did not think she would have to register so soon and had not got on the land already, and as she is a cook. Stella[32] thinks they will put her in the Services where she would really be serving her country better.[33] Stella does not know what to do as her husband is in the Midlands with a Home Guard job, both the children are away, and she won't have any petrol to go to Dorchester to do WVS work. She thinks of shutting up the house except for weekends and living in Dorchester but it will be very lonely for Kathleen and Peter if she does, without any neighbours at all.

Saturday, April 11. Talked to Ruth Grundy, who was also staying there, about next term. She seems more apprehensive now and is wondering how she would get on with Miss Bennett. I think she will calm down the intenseness a bit, which will be a good thing. She said that Miss Bennett had been bombed out twice so no wonder she seems a bit on edge by the end of the term. Kathleen's old maid and nurse help who joined the WAAF had been home on leave and seems very happy, but most of the time was spent in ringing up or taking messages from her boy who is trying to meet her.

Sunday, April 12. Peter had a day out with the Home Guard and came back to take us back to Blandford. He says they cannot go on much longer doing all this on Sundays and working so hard all the week. He says the countryman has no idea of the urgency of the war at all. They were thrashing the other day with other farmers all round, all waiting for the thrasher, and because he was called away the team stopped with half an hour's work to do and the whole thing had to be started up the next morning for that little bit and a day's work wasted. Came away after tea and left John behind until next weekend in floods of tears.

Monday, April 13. Typed some more instructions about Buttercup Day. Issued wool vouchers and sorted needlework at the WVS. Went on with my shirts after lunch. Gay looked in to fix up about going to Bournemouth tomorrow and stayed all the afternoon. Did my washing and went on with needlework and a bit of gardening.

Tuesday, April 14. Went down to Bournemouth on the 10.05 bus, which was crowded but a nice little school girl offered me her seat and she got off half way. We shopped till 1 and met the boy and girl Gay had brought with her and ate our lunch on the front, which was lovely. I went off and finished my shopping and joined them at the pictures to see *Dr. Jekyll and Mr. Hyde.* I had not seen a film for ages and I enjoyed it very much. We had tea afterwards and missed the bus home. For once I did not have to worry, not having a child to put to bed, but Gay had left someone with hers and said she would get home by 6.15. We took the next bus to Wimborne, hoping that the Poole bus would be late and that the Blandford bus would have to wait for it.

---

[32] Wife of Brigadier Charles H. Woodhouse.

[33] In order to release male farm workers for military service, women were being called up for agricultural labour, usually in the Women's Land Army, which was one of the approved organizations in which able-bodied unmarried women could perform their national service.

However, we had no luck. I had no intention of walking and could wait for the 7.45 but we decided to try and hitch hike. The boy walked on one road and we all waited at the cross roads. After a bit Gay said she would go back and try and borrow a bike, so she left us and after one false start we stopped a car driven by the local Member of Parliament,[34] whose family very kindly squashed up to nothing and we came home very comfortably. Gay lent the girl my bike and she got down the road very quickly and I met the friend who had stayed and put the children to bed and she said Gay had rung up and said she was biking so I did not worry. As we finished listening to the news, in walked Gay and the boy, having walked all but 1½ miles. She could not borrow a bike and had rung up on her way to look for it. She thought she had better take the same road as the boy so had not been overtaken by the bus and had only had a short lift.

Wednesday, April 15. Sorted needlework at the WVS. Another awful muddle of knitting from Milton Abbas. Balaclava helmet made in precious RAF scarf wool and socks made from khaki scarf wool. Looked at the bees in the afternoon. One lot queenless but all the others very well with lots of brood and stores. I wish my sugar would come. Went on with shirts and pyjamas in the evening.

24. Balaclava and mittens, knitted from a wartime pattern

Friday, April 17. Went to Melcombe to fetch John home. He had been terribly homesick, which was not at all according to plan and knocks on the head the plan I had of sending him as a boarder at his school for a week or two in September. I sat in the kitchen all the morning and talked to my sister while she cooked. They have no

[34] Rt. Hon. Captain Angus V. Hambro, M.P. for North Dorset.

wireless at the moment and their paper is a day late. I slept out at my cousin's, who was away, but a friend was there and we talked until after midnight. She has a married daughter in Burma – at least she and her nurse and children are now in Calcutta but the husband is fighting in Burma and she is desperate for them both and listens to every news bulletin in the hopes of some sort of reassurance. She was glad to have someone fresh to tell it all to and to talk about her beloved only daughter.

Saturday, April 18. Kathleen's nurse had a half day and the maid always takes the opportunity to ask for extra time off when I go there so we had a busy time, but very pleasant, so far from the war. Peter had been into Dorchester market and his car broke down with a burst tyre. He could only get a new inner tube from his usual garage at a village half way in but the bus would not take the tube into the town because it was after 6. He had to come out by the last bus and we shall have to hire to get home tomorrow.

Sunday, April 19. After several ringings up by us and the garage we got home by car and bus in time for tea. We had to leave John's precious bike behind to come in with Kathleen next week.

Monday, April 20. The typewriter at the WVS has gone mysteriously wrong and the ribbon will not stay in position. It is a pity the Scotch nurse who had been in an insurance office has gone because she could always save the situation. Asked my Father if he knew of anyone who could mend it. Did the week's washing in the afternoon and went down to the Killicks for tea.

Tuesday, April 21. Father says the assistant secretary in the office thinks he can put the typewriter right if Mrs. Stuart can bring it down. Packed up the last batch of needlework and labelled all the piles of different work, ready to show someone else the ropes presently. Watched the soldiers playing with their amphibian tank again. They have brought some chess-pale [*i.e. chestnut paling*] fencing and stout stakes and made a firm bottom to the landing place. An old man came over and watched and called to mind when he was a lad that he had taken horses and carts into the river at the ford many a time, and there was a firm enough bottom to it then. They tried the tank afterwards but it was no better and they had to haul it out with a wire rope again. Went down the river meadows to get kingcups and look for nests. Finished my last boy's shirt before the *Brains Trust*.[35]

Saturday, April 25. We had a lot of planes over in the night. I suppose the summer raids have begun.[36] It sounded as if they were going to Bristol, as usual, but the first news did not say so. When I heard so many on their way somewhere else I settled off to sleep but our poor evacuee was rather miserable. However, she is a floor lower and now she sleeps with the invalid so she knows we are all around if anything does

---

[35] The *Brains Trust* was a popular quiz programme on the wireless, featuring a panel made up of both resident 'brains' and invited guests.

[36] This was the week when the so-called Baedeker Raids began against five historic cities – Canterbury, Norwich, Exeter, York, and Bath. Details are provided in Niall Rothnie, *The Baedeker Blitz: Hitler's Attack on Britain's Historic Cities* (Shepperton, Surrey: Ian Allan, 1992).

happen. I went down to hear where it was at 7 but it could not have been Coventry again from what they said, so J.R. will be alright.

Monday, April 27. Fancy it's being Bath [being bombed]. Father is worried about his friends there but the Stuarts were very worried about their old cook who was spending a holiday there with friends. The General has his new set of dentures there too and Mrs. Stuart a new coat and skirt. They tried to get through about the cook but even the police could not help.

Tuesday, April 28. The cook turned up by the Black and White – alright but very shaken.[37] She spent most of the day in bed but had told them the night before of most of the damage. The house she was in was alright and they stayed under the stairs. No news of the Taylors and rumour has it that their district and the dentist's has got it badly. I told Mrs. Stuart that I should have to give up working for her and suggested Joan T. as a successor. She thought it a good idea and said she would ask herself at the British Restaurant on Friday. I packed a lot of pyjamas and other garments to be stored against emergency for the hospital.

Wednesday, April 29. Mrs. H., who is housing the hospital things, came up to Letton to point out that the invoice did not agree with her checking. That is my fault because in my agitation at breaking the news to Mrs. Stuart, I did not countercheck when I packed. Mrs. Stuart was really put out, which she never is when it is ordinary WVS work, but she minds about the hospital and when her civic reputation is at stake.[38]

Thursday, April 30. Had a day at home and turned out the nursery. Ruth Grundy turned up. She seems to be getting on fairly well at John's school but has to teach older ones than she is used to and finds them rather lazy. She likes the staff, however, and it will be alright when she has got into the swing of it. Went up to Dr. Wilson and got my milk and coupon forms. He said they were rather loath to issue coupons until the sixth month of pregnancy but I will see if I can get them sooner or I shall never get through. Took John to the dentist to have a stopping put in again.

Friday, May 1. Father had a short letter from his friend in Bath. They are alright. All the windows broken but they think they can patch the house up enough for the

[37] Black and White Motorways Ltd. operated long-distance coach services from their base in Cheltenham.

[38] Mrs Stuart was a local magistrate. Her husband was Treasurer of the Hospital.

summer at any rate. She is at rather a low ebb. The Stuarts had a letter from friends who had spent the night in a trench in the park with high explosives falling all around. Their house was standing but all the doors had been blown in by the blast.[39] Mrs. Stuart had thought out a way of squaring the mistake in the invoice without having to alter matron's list.

Saturday, May 2. My birthday. Several letters, including an airgraph from my sister in India.[40] Ruth Grundy sold me some coupon free material she had got some time ago from a friend of a friend in the trade. It will come in very usefully for a smock. Wrote to Dorchester for my coupons and said that I was working for the WVS. I had very little time for sewing or knitting and would be very glad if I could have them, as pregnancy was established without a doubt.

Monday, May 4. The typewriter is mended and just in time as there were notices to send out to the Rest Centres on the care of hot water bottles and to the representatives about taking on the interviewing of 16 year olds under the Registration of Youth.[41] Joan T. says she will come up and look at the job and is quite keen to take it on.

Tuesday, May 5. Joan came up and was not at all intimidated and will take it on, but she won't be able to do up the parcels or to do writing in the very cold weather as her circulation is so bad and she has no strength in partly paralysed arms then. She did some typing and that was alright. She stands up to do it but gets it done. Went up to the milk office to get my permit and met my sister getting fruit juice in there. We had a nice matey time with people in there. Mrs. H. has two children at expensive schools who are huge for their ages and she has great trouble with their clothes so that her husband is in rags and she is very shabby, but she says the uniforms are very good and really do last. We chatted round the town and I helped her buy her rations and points but the grocer had all his dried fruit taken for the Camp by NAAFI so she could only get prunes.

Wednesday, May 6. Sold buttercups for the crippled children. Cut out a smock from the stuff I bought from Ruth Grundy.

---

[39] The damage caused to Bath by these raids is described in Rothnie's *Baedeker Blitz*, pp. 49–73, and in his earlier book, *The Bombing of Bath: The German Air Raids of April 1942* (Bath: Ashgrove Press, 1983). Most houses in the city sustained some damage, even if only a few broken windows; some 329 houses were completely destroyed and at least 1,000 others were made uninhabitable. Around 400 people lost their lives. This was just the sort of crisis in which the WVS became especially active. 'In Bath the WVS Centre escaped damage, although both the Organiser and her deputy lost their homes. The Housewives section were mobilised and did valuable work in 27 emergency feeding centres at which 20,000 meals were served in one day. The destruction of several Rest Centres in the city made the work of dealing with the homeless even more urgent, and Rest Centres in the surrounding outlying districts were opened. WVS cars took many people to Bristol and other places where they had relatives.' (*WVS Bulletin*, no. 32, June 1942, p. 1.)

[40] This sister was Christine Huthwaite, the youngest of the four Woodhouse sisters.

[41] In 1942 a government directive ordered that all people should be interviewed and registered for National Service on reaching the age of 16.

A few days before Phyllis had responded to a question from Mass-Observation concerning clothes and rationing, and her answer sheds some light on significant constraints, both before and during the war

> For a good many years now my clothing has been ruled by my purse rather than by my inclination and I really welcomed clothes rationing because it enabled me to economise without feeling conspicuous. I can now wear good lasting clothes every day instead of buying less expensively so that I shall have several different lots of clothes to appear in. I dress in very much the same colours that I have always done but I accept anything offered gratefully. I stopped changing for the evening in the cold winter but I shall be able to change my underclothes twice a week in spite of the soap rationing as I have always done. I have given up wearing evening dress altogether and do not even possess one now. I do not think I spend more on clothes. I should think my wardrobe has increased slightly because I give nothing away but keep [them] in case things get worse or I might be able to make the garment into something else. *(Directive Response, April 1942.)*

Thursday, May 7. Mrs. Oliver has sent Ruth to John's school this term and her husband [a doctor] finishes his round there twice a week and says he will bring them back and she will drive them down those days. This is a grand idea and will help to wean John from the maternal apron string. Joan suggested Miss M. could take the store of clothes for the town Rest Centres. Her house is within the tank island and big enough to have spare attics. Wrote and asked her to do this. Went to Infant Welfare and did the files, which is very dull. The new welfare worker has come and was being shown round. She has come from Southampton and finds so many different local clinics difficult to get the hang of after working in one building all the time. Gay had an appointment with the chiropodist so dropped Richard in to play with John while I was out. The gardener told them to stay in the garden but they escaped to the weir – but happily with no dangerous results. Went to the office and typed after supper and the night watchman, who is an ex-naval man, told me that it was only just by luck he had not sent his best false leg off to be done up. He had a bit of digging he had not got done or it would have been bombed in Exeter.[42]

Friday, May 8. Miss M. came and said she would take the clothes if we would keep them until the end of the week as she is at work all day and would have to clean up the room a bit first.

Saturday, May 9. Joseph May came to take away the little bit of furniture we are sending to a friend in London who is starting a flat. One of the men was the same as the lot who brought it all down but he did not remember it. They were not nearly so efficient a team as the others so I'm glad we had not a big load to go off. They said

[42] Exeter had been targeted by German bombers during two nights in April (the 23rd and 24th), and was heavily damaged by raids on the night of May 3rd.

they had such trouble over food now there were no travellers' ration books. They never knew how long a job would take them and they were nearly always in the country away from British Restaurants. They were going on to Bournemouth so they would be alright for once but they asked me for a small bottle which would hold a half pint of milk. Went up to the Down House to view the sale there. The house was burnt down in parts more than a year ago but they had rescued a good bit and what was not being sold in London or bought by the family is to be sold on Monday and Tuesday. John very much wanted an egg cabinet with some old eggs collected by Mr. J. when he was a boy and I would like some of the oriental bowls if I can get them. Father viewed yesterday and is getting someone to bid for the pictures for a memento. Our evacuee came up too by bus and has her eye on a lot. She got a lift back, which was very lucky.[43]

25. The Down House, photographed before the war

Monday, May 11. Went up to the sale after WVS, where there was very little doing. John is parked on the Killicks. My china went too dear but I bid for several lots. I did a deal for the cabinet for John and paid a dealer 10s for it and he delivered it for me. There were a lot of local dealers there but not many from London except a Jew who they all disliked, and he was tricky with the bidding,[44] but the auctioneer was a bit past it and as the reception rooms had been burnt there was nowhere they could carry lots

[43] The estate up for auction was that of the late Sir John R.W. Smith-Marriott.

[44] There is much evidence from wartime diaries, and from other documents in the Mass-Observation Archive, that disdain for Jews was commonplace in English society. Later revelations of Nazi atrocities helped to change these views. These issues are explored in Tony Kushner, *The Persistence of Prejudice: Anti-Semitism in British Society during the Second World War* (Manchester University Press, 1989).

and we had to walk round the rooms with him. Poor little Miss Smith did not get a look in and to make matters worse she had to walk back and took the wrong turning as she came out so that she was halfway to Dorchester before she discovered her mistake. She would never have got lost in a town but the country seems a mystery she cannot fathom. I don't think Father got any of his lots. Nothing was going very cheap although no one seemed to be buying just for the sake of it. He went rook shooting and got quite a nice lot but the nettles were awful and the ground very rough and he cannot shoot so well when he has to stand with a steady gun instead of snap shooting walking along.

Tuesday, May 12. Had the Killicks to tea so that Gay could go to the sale. She had a good afternoon and bought several outside lots, which make her a home from home. I noted the dealer who had bought Miss Smith's lot and she has written to him to know if he will part with an ancestral foot bath.

Wednesday, May 13. Miss Smith had a letter to say she can have it for 7s 6d so she is in raptures. Her old invalid is having bouts of being very troublesome and crotchety but she bears with her wonderfully.

Thursday, May 14. My coupons have come without any fuss so now we will have a shopping day and Father says we can have the big car for probably the last time as it will be laid by in June.

Friday, May 15. We had a good day in Bournemouth and got all we wanted. I forgot to take a case when I went to buy napkins for the baby and had to walk down to the car carrying them in hand, but there, who cares? I got my husband a new pair of Jaeger slippers for Christmas out of the coupons and some blue wool for stockings for John to wear at school. We could not get our watches mended. I let Mother go in with them as she knew the man when they were all young but he told her the same tale as I have had twice so we shall just have to manage.

Saturday, May 16. We took the clothes up to Miss M. in the firm's little van. We did not have to carry them up to the top of the house which was a great relief as I had carried them down from ours. I have just got rid of them in time because Dorchester wrote to tell me they were bringing me a new consignment soon. They are now getting all the warm coats and gloves they were meant to get last winter.

Monday, May 18. Undid parcels of work up at the WVS. We seem very rich so have sent for more patterns of stuff for dressing gowns and pyjamas. Met the VADs [nurses] at the casual ward in the afternoon to prepare tins for the Red Cross Flag Day. We got on so well that we set out all the rural boxes and flags ready to be taken away during the week. They are going to have another white elephant sale for their funds.

Wednesday, May 20. The Southern Command have begun their manoeuvres round here. When John and I were waiting for Ruth Oliver for school some lorries arrived and parked in the road to the garages and camouflaged their lorries. Father and the gardener saw the aeroplanes go by and drop parachutists. He saw them land and run into the side of the hedge but when I went up to the WVS I saw one captured. There were men hiding with their guns all along the Salisbury Road. After school we had a 2 lb anti-aircraft gun in the road and all the cover by the bridge was hiding troops and guns. The referee was there too. John spent his day with them.

Thursday, May 21. John out first thing and brought up a dish for us to make tea for one of his pals. Mrs. Stuart has had a communication from headquarters asking how much Merchant Navy wool we will undertake to knit up in eight weeks. We have also heard from London asking for all the RAF wool we had to be returned. Some of this has only just gone out. Wrote to everybody and asked them to return what they had. Infant Welfare in the afternoon. I had to weigh the babies, which is great fun. There are some nice babies coming now, only two slummy ones the whole afternoon, and they were not nearly as dirty as their mothers. A lot of them are first babies, which accounts for their beautiful clothes perhaps but not for their grand bodies. Lots of them belong to soldiers' wives who have been to clinics wherever they have been. I wonder if they find it a way of making friends or if they feel they need the advice. Came home to find the bridge just about to be blown up. Crowds of small boys running backwards and forwards in great excitement, my own among them. A soldier came and asked us to make them some tea, which we did in a jug as for haymakers. In the course of conversation we found he was the enemy and the town had been taken in the morning by paratroops. We went out and saw the blowing up of the bridge and then our gun went off but more troops arrived to guard something and asked Mother a lot of questions which she answered before she thought they were the enemy – and we have just been having lectures to make us invasion conscious. Still, they all talked to us in such familiar Cockney and I don't think the Germans will manage that.

Friday, May 22. Rachel came this morning saying she had found a Royal Army Service Corps motorcyclist in the little road last night who had lost his party and, having seen two men killed, had thought he would take things quietly until it was time to close down. He had had no rations so she gave him her thermos of tea which she makes and takes home each night to have before she starts in the morning. When we went to school he was fast asleep by the river. Ruth Oliver came to tea with John. They rode round the garden the whole time on their bikes. The soldiers had all done by dinner time, for which I was glad, as Ruth's mother might not have cared for her to sit and worship them too.[45]

Saturday, May 23. We moved John to the nursery to sleep by himself and we spent the very wet day in the loft looking for a bedside table for him. He was very happy about it, especially as he has the little clock, and we unpacked our big clock to stand on my chest of drawers. Its chime is quite mad – I don't want that on at night – but it does keep time and is our last hope until the end of the war.

---

[45] A dance at the Corn Exchange in aid of the Cottage Hospital – 'music being provided by a military band' – was held this evening and got coverage in the press. 'Attendance was good; in fact, men outnumbered women. The hall was prettily decorated. . .. Refreshments were dispensed by VAD nurses in uniform, the takings from which were devoted to the Linen Guild. The sum of £43 has been handed to General Stuart, treasurer of the hospital, as the proceeds of the dance, and the Linen Guild benefited by £10.' (*Dorset County Chronicle*, 28 May 1942, p. 5.)

Monday, May 25. Some of the RAF wool was returned not made up by the working parties, which is a blow as there is not much time for anyone in the summer and now we have all promised to get the Merchant Navy knitting done. They sent over my new batch of clothing and we asked Mrs. S., who brought it, to stay for tea. She was an interesting person but like my Mrs. Stuart quite out of her element working in a world of women. She is well off and has now had to register and will be called up because although she does 37 hours of voluntary work it is not all in one organisation. They offered her a trade job driving a van at £3 a week. It does seem difficult. What she likes best is entertaining the troops and was going off tonight to recite to a concert at M_____. She married at 21 and had four children in five years and her husband is a Conservative Member of Parliament and she seems to be living apart and not in charge of the children but she dislikes Americans and is a Vansittart as far as I could gather.[46] It's nice to have as much milk as we like again.[47]

Tuesday, May 26. The patterns came from the Personal Service League for the pyjamas and dressing gowns we intend to make. The stuff gets worse and worse. There was nothing fit to make up for men's dressing gowns but [there was] some moderate pyjama material and some winceyette for children. I am glad we had not thought of shirts because that was worse than anything. Father went for his blood transfusion and suffered no ill effects. We have not been told where and when but I shall not do it this time. I could not lie down on the horrid little stretchers in the public view even if I could spare the blood. Rachel says she won't give hers again because she has so many sties on her eyes since. Took John to tea with Mrs. Oliver and he and Ruth had a happy time while we did our knitting in the sitting room and discussed schools etc. Dr. Oliver came into tea after doing his grapes. He made £16 last year and got 1s each from his peaches too, but in peacetime he gives them away. They were going down to the elder child's school for the weekend. They chose the school because it had such palatial grounds and is in such a safe district and now, with petrol difficulties, they wonder how much time they will have to spend with the child as it is so far from where they will stay.

Wednesday, May 27. We had our blood transfusion notices today. They said blood was urgently needed for Libya so Rachel is reconsidering her decision as her boy must have had a transfusion when he was wounded. We had letters from India. Christine is now senior lady as there are two bachelors over her husband. She finds it very difficult to talk to the native officers and women as she can really only give orders in Urdhu. She has been giving lectures to the native wives in first aid and now has found another wife who has been a nurse and is very proficient in the language as well as knowing Indians very well so it is much better. Christine finds she was giving them much more than they could take in. We are all becoming rabbit conscious and thinking of joining

---

[46] It is possible, though not certain, that this woman's husband was James Gray Stuart, MP for Moray and Nairn since 1923, who lived at Redlynch near Salisbury. Baron Vansittart of Denham (b.1881), a former diplomat and senior civil servant and member of the House of Lords since 1941, saw Germany as inherently aggressive and barbaric, and advocated through his speeches and writing a tough-minded treatment of Germany after her defeat.

[47] As an expectant mother, she was entitled to a pint of milk a day.

the rabbit club. Gay Killick has decided to have a young doe [female] that the children can play with and a mated doe to have a family soon. It is not nearly so expensive to start as *Picture Post* gave me to understand but the hutches seem to have to be much larger than the ordinary cottage size.

This is one of the rare occasions when Phyllis mentioned reading. Mass-Observation's Directive for this month asked about people's reading habits, and she returned the following answer.

The only books I read regularly are *Picture Post* [actually, a magazine], which I send to my sister in Australia for her birthday and Christmas presents, the *New Statesman*, which she gives me for my presents, and *Reader's Digest*, which my Father takes in. I used to belong to Boots Library but I found I took so long to read a book that I might as well buy it. I sometimes take out a book from there on my Mother's subscription. My husband was a member of the Left Book Club before the war and I brought all those books down with me and read them slowly, and also a friend sent her books down with our furniture and I read them, especially any new ones in the Readers Union, of which she was a member. When I stay with my sister, who is literary, I borrow something of hers I feel I ought to have read long ago. If she has finished her library book and wants me to take it back and change it, I read that and my parents' library books if they are out and I think they are interesting or by authors I like, or I have read reviews of them.[48]

She indicated that 'I only buy books to give children and when somebody gives me a book token'.

I read less and less and nearly all political stuff. I feel I must know more about how to run the world so I can struggle to make a better one for my children. In my own home I rarely listened to the wireless except the news or when I was doing needlework as I can read and knit at the same time. Now one of us always wants the programme on the wireless and I always have something I must get done so that I do not go to bed early and read there. I read to my small boy for the quarter of an hour in the morning between making myself a cup of tea and getting up, except on Sunday when I read to myself for a half hour. When we had another maid and I did no housework I could read like this every day. (*Directive Response, May 1942*.)

Thursday, May 28. Had the day off as the Stuarts were going to see the remains of their dentures in Bath. There were oranges on the town, free for all, as they are the small dry kind. We were able to have 2 lbs and they are not at all bad. The Red Cross

[48] She is talking about subscription libraries, where there was a charge for borrowing.

had their white elephant stall but there was such a queue of back-laners waiting for the doors to open that I did not go in.[49] Little Miss Smith went and got a minute teapot and a home-made cake, which she thought were fine bargains. I have decided not to have a rabbit until after September as John is not really keen and if he took it over to my sister's the dogs or cats would be sure to get it.

Friday, May 29. The Killicks came to tea and we went to see someone's rabbits. They seem to be getting on alright but say they take a lot of feeding and cleaning out. They had two bucks, two does, one with very young and the other just separated from hers, which were all in a big hutch which could be made into two.

Monday, June 1. I was asked to supply clothes for a small boy evacuee living on a farm and helping with the work. He only brought good clothes with him and has no coupons left. We had a pair of shorts in the secondhand, which were the [right] size, and with the help of some odd coupons which had to be taken for some baby clothes Mrs. Stuart had bought before rationing, I could supply the boots. We heard from Christine in India. She had been receiving and marrying off a bride who had escaped from Singapore and been just two days ahead of the Japs all the way.[50] Ruth Oliver came to tea with John. They rode their bicycles round the paths the whole time. Gay Killick came with her children to fetch an old run for her rabbits. She had asked the farmer's daughter who came with waste paper to fetch it for her but she could not manage it on the cart. However, she brought a wonderful barrow made by her husband and by having the run partly over her head managed to get it down the road. Dr. Oliver may be called up as Dorset has to supply so many more doctors and Blandford is not as badly off as some other towns. The locum would like to go but has gastric ulcer and they won't take any more with that kind of trouble.

Tuesday, June 2. My last day at the WVS. Mrs. Stuart was longer than ever over housekeeping so that we were rushed going through the books and the needlework as it was my day for fetching the children from school. It saved a lot of polite words at the end as I had to rush off. I think they will get on without any trouble. Charles[51] came over on his bicycle. He is on leave from running the Home Guard in the Midlands. He is liking it very much. The men are many of them in reserved occupations, so wonderful soldiers, and many of them wish they were unreserved and [could] put all they have into the job. He was surprised to find the black market so much more rife up there than down here or in Plymouth, where he was before. He said it was worth going to London just to see St. Paul's in its new setting.[52]

---

49 The residents of Back Lane, now Bryanston Street, had a reputation for feckless and disorderly ways.

50 Singapore had fallen to the Japanese in February.

51 Brigadier Charles Woodhouse, OBE, MC, of Higher Melcombe, near Ansty. He was first cousin to Phyllis. He had a distinguished military career in the First World War, and took command of the Home Guard (Midlands) in 1941 as General Staff Officer (information from Julian Walther).

52 She is presumably referring to the fact that St. Paul's was now surrounded by bomb-destroyed buildings.

Wednesday, June 3. Sold flags for the Red Cross and then did needlework until it was time to fetch the children. M.[53] came in to see if I had lost a swarm of bees as he had one in his garden which he did not think was his. I looked at it and saw it wasn't mine and watched him take it and arranged to see him run it in the evening. Had a picnic by the river with the Killicks. The bees went off and left the skep and went into a hole in a high tree.[54] We all felt very sad as it was bad news in Russia.[55]

26. Oliver 'Twisty' Turner making bee-skeps at Thornicombe, Blandford St. Mary in 1941

Thursday, June 4. Went through my hives to see who was going to swarm. Went to Infant Welfare in the afternoon and to tea at the Olivers where I had left John to play with Ruth. They are not going to have a holiday this year as they cannot go to the Isle of Wight where they always went. He only likes messing about in boats and cannot think of anything else he would like to do. Came home early as Kathleen was coming in to get her stores. Went into town with her and picked up those – also some tomatoes and a wireless set which is finished at last. Met a friend who had come in on a late bus not realising that the shops shut at 6 or before, and she got in too late for a lift back. Tried to get sweets but they seem very short until the rationing comes into force.

---

[53] Jim Mantell, Head Maltster at the Brewery. He lived in the Head Brewer's House next to Old Ford House (information from Julian Walther).

[54] A skep is a straw or wicker beehive. 'Bees are still kept in skeps made of straw, or reeds, or of osiers plastered with mud and cow-dung, in hollow logs, in earthenware pipes, and in wooden boxes,' according to a contemporary authority, 'but the modern movable frame hive has practically superseded all the earlier types. Straw skeps are convenient for taking swarms and as a temporary housing for them. Their use occasionally enters into modern systems, but owing to the difficulty of controlling disease with hives with fixed combs, the use of skeps, boxes and the like as permanent hives is poor practice, and indeed in many places is prohibited by law.' (E.B. Wedmore, *A Manual of Bee-Keeping for English-speaking Bee-keepers* [London, 2nd edn., 1945], p. 163.)

[55] German forces were bombarding Sevastopol.

Friday, June 5. My bees swarmed but the queen crawled up the leg of the spare hive and did not have to be taken in a skep. Another swarm appeared on the railing, which we took to be mine too, but in the end I thought it must be M's come out of the tree, and anyhow I was glad to give him the benefit of the doubt as he is such a help when J.R. isn't here, and I gave him the bars for his hive so now we are all square and I can drag him down from the vat room [in the brewery] to help me if need be. We were in such a way with swarms all over the place that I had to ask H.F. to tea as I had no time to take John there and he is too shy to go alone. She had made a cake for tea so she brought it with her. They had a dull time as she can't mount her bike unaided and, being a bit tongue tied, John cannot understand one word she says. I saw M. run his bees in and the queen was well in front. Bees are nice to deal with. They seem so sane and well organised when the world seems hastening to its doom.

Saturday, June 6. The Home Guard had another exercise all night – at least it seemed to be over by 10. They seemed to lose the brewery to the enemy.

Sunday, June 7. Heard more about the Home Guard exercise. The Red Cross people were captured by the Germans, who shut them all up in one room and would not let any of them go home. The officer in charge really acted up to his role and told them they were all dead as he was taking no prisoners. There seems to be some conflicting opinions about the capture as others said that the First Aid people were supposed to move inside the tank island after 9 and that was why they were captured, which was very awkward as there was no one to attend to the wounded. One of the sergeants spotted a fifth columnist[56] dressed as a policeman who had gone into the police station and been accepted as a colleague. He spotted him because there was something wrong about his collar and he arrested him just before he threw a bomb.

Monday, June 8. Did ironing and gardening in the morning. John and I took the Killicks' tomatoes grown in our greenhouse down to them[57] and walked back with Ruth Grundy on her way home from school. They had Home Guard through their garden and smoke bombs and altogether an exciting time. Went to the Killicks in the evening to sit there while Gay went to fetch a rabbit.

Tuesday, June 9. Met Joan T. They seem to be getting on very well up at Letton but the voucher we issued for coupon free wool on a new ration book was disallowed and they must still use the odd bit of the old clothing card. Went into the town with John to choose his prize. I tried to bribe him to go into school without playing up and clinging to my hand as if I was going away forever. He won it so easily that I felt rather done, especially as I had to pay 5s for the box of powder paints he chose. Richard Killick came to tea and they spent a blissful time messing about and in the end painting each other's faces.

Wednesday, June 10. I had to keep John from school as he complained of swollen glands. He did not seem ill at all and I let him play with the charwoman's little girl out

---

[56] The term 'fifth column' was widely used in Britain in the Second World War to describe (supposed) secret supporters of the Nazi and Fascist movements.

[57] These must be tomato plants. Tomatoes do not fruit in this country until late summer.

of doors. I don't think it can be either scarlet fever or chicken pox. I turned out the nursery and wrote letters and cut out the new baby's nightdresses in the afternoon. Gay Killick came in for a bath after the British Restaurant and Ruth Grundy came in to tea on her way home from school. She says Miss Bennett, who takes John's form, is sickening for something and is only on her feet by a miracle.

Thursday, June 11. John quite alright and back at school. Made a start on the nightdresses. Made bee frames for the honey supers.[58] Took John for a ride in the evening.

Friday, June 12. Rather wet day. Took John to tea at the F's. Not a great success as he and H. don't get on and we could not really talk. The General has been bowler hatted[59] but does not mind very much as his job was being converted to women. He said they came down on the administrative side. His wife said she did not know what would happen about his batman as they had been together for 25 years and really could not get on without each other. There was some hope of the batman being discharged on medical grounds as he had pleurisy every winter, but that was doubtful.

Saturday, June 13. We had a decent bee day at last and I went through all the hives. The honey is coming in nicely but not into sections. If only we have a good month now all will be well. John and I had a bicycle ride in the evening – always the same way, where there are no hills. Father listened to the Derby. Rachel had a shilling on both ways and spotted the winner.

Sunday, June 14. Went to the parade in the town for United Nations Day. Not a great crowd there. A band from the Camp and detachments of ATS and Royal Artillery as well as air cadets and local cadets from the schools and Home Guard, Girl Guides, ARP and Air Defence Sector. The service was poor because no one thought to put the loud speakers on until halfway through, but it was something to go to.

Monday, June 15. Letters from Australia. Apparently Americans are being distributed through the houses but Isabel says she has not got any yet. I should think it doubtful if she could find room for them. They are said to be very nice. She had had a shopping day in Melbourne and met people she had known in India. Clothes she said were terribly expensive – lisle stockings 8s 6d a pair and a Chilprufe vest 17s. She heard from her husband in India that he would have to go and live at the club if petrol got any shorter, which makes it difficult for her as she had intended to go back when the children were nicely settled in boarding schools. There are plenty of people she knows who will be kind to them in the holidays. There is a men's haircutting crisis in Blandford. One man has died and his assistant called up for munitions and only two shops for the whole population.

Tuesday, June 16. Miss Bennett, John's form mistress, has collapsed at last with what sounds like nervous dyspepsia. They have got the ex-head of a little school who gave up after a nervous breakdown, and she has had several since, but perhaps she will

---

[58] A super is a box containing a certain number of sections of honey.

[59] Retired from the forces.

last out the term. The back tyre of John's bike burst this afternoon, happily when he was in the garden. I thought the gardener was shooting a rat – it was such a loud report. I went up to the bicycle shop and managed to buy the last two tyres and inner tubes he had in that size. It seemed so queer to only pay 11s for something so terribly precious. We are all terribly depressed by the bad news from Libya. It is the first time we have been really down.[60] Even Dunkirk and Singapore made very little difference and we just said – well, we must expect awful news. I think the wave of optimism which has swept the country has influenced us more than we thought, although we read the *New Statesman* and the *K.H. News Letter*, which ought to keep our minds balanced.[61]

Wednesday, June 17. Went up to the florist's to see if my long ordered dahlias had turned up but the husband was out and I chatted to his wife, who had just registered and felt that a mild job in a munition factory would be heaven compared to her job. 'It isn't just the selling things but one day you think you will get the washing done and no sooner have you got going when someone will come in for wreaths and there is no one to do them but yourself and they must be done.' They are the last thing I would be bothered with in wartime but I suppose they are the only paying thing left in their business. Went down to the Killicks and watched the farmer making hay. The children pitched up the bits that fell off the elevator. The team was wonderful. Three very old age pensioners and one horse and a little engine to work the elevator, which took a long time to start up. They loaded all three carts and left them by the rick and then started the engine and made the rick. None of the farmers round here avail themselves of the Women's Land Army because they don't want to pay anyone and really these old men, who all knew what they were doing although not one of them had been a farm labourer, got on with the job as quickly as it could be done with the equipment provided.

Thursday, June 18. Infant Welfare again. The town nurse comes now and does the baby weighing, which does me out of the nicest job, but I was able to ask her about a soldier's wife who applied for a layette. I have been questioning them myself but this time I came to the conclusion that it was time that they came to me through the Soldiers', Sailors' and Airmen's Families Association welfare officer as, although she is bedridden, she knows more about the townspeople than anyone else. The nurse thought she should have one without any doubt. We noticed that so many of the toddlers are losing weight and blame it on double summer time as it is certain that they are getting less sleep than they should be.[62]

Friday, June 19. Mrs. W. came in about clothes for two children in her village. One is an orphan whose aunt only gets 5s a week to keep her on, and this leaves very little to dress her with, and the other is one of a large family where the mother has been very ill. They both had plenty of coupons. Mrs. W. has been a world's worker and investigates her cases very carefully herself, which is so much easier for

---

[60] British forces were retreating in the face of German attacks, and Tobruk was threatened. The military situation in North Africa looked bleak.

[61] The *K-H News Letter*, published weekly, was produced by Stephen King-Hall.

[62] Since the clock was put forward two hours, daylight in June lasted for most of the evening.

27. Haymaking in Blandford St. Mary, 1940

me than the lady bountiful who would like to take everything and antagonize the village people.

Saturday, June 20. Spent the day in needlework and gardening, trying to get the nightdresses finished before Rachel goes for her holiday. Mrs. Stuart brought down some odd crystals to put among the clothing in the store to keep out moths. Someone said it smelt just like French railway carriages and it made them homesick for foreign travel.

Monday, June 22. Rachel away for a fortnight. She registers on Saturday but as she does not want to go we can try and get her off for a bit – anyway, until September is over. I shall get up a bit more punctually and be down so soon after 7 and get the dining room and hall done as well as what I usually do before breakfast. I shan't turn out any rooms and I ought to be through by 11.

Tuesday, June 23. We have got on very well without Rachel but I hope it won't be for always. It is very different doing this old fashioned house from our cottage.[63] It seems to matter so if you leave anything undone here. I suppose it has been so well kept for so long.

Wednesday, June 24. We had another application from the ATS for clothes for a girl being discharged and coming from Southern Ireland. Again I was able to fit her up very well with a frock and a coat but as the coat was rather thin she had a little green

[63] She is presumably referring to the house in Delcombe where she lived for a while after leaving London in 1939.

jacket to go under it, which went very well with the green silk frock which had just come in. We had a nice picnic by the river with Ruth Grundy and Mrs. Oliver, Ruth Oliver and John. Dr. P., an old friend of my Father's, came to dinner and we did him quite well with spring chicken, new potatoes and peas, stewed blackcurrants and junket, cheese savoury, and burgundy to drink. He is an Air Raid Warden and told about the bad raids in Poole the other day. He said it really was terrifying, with the dive bombers coming down for three solid hours, and absolutely miraculous that they did so little damage. They did hit the pipeline of the petrol store and set the brewery on fire, under which was a huge shelter which they had planned to make into an emergency hospital, but it was flooded with water putting the fire out.[64]

Thursday, June 25. J.R. rang up and said he would bring the car down to put up for the duration, arriving about 11. Father had bridge so I sat and played patience and kept a meal hot for him. He did not come until after 2 and I had turned the hot plate out soon after 1 but the meal was alright. He had a beard and looked pure Bloomsbury until he was washed.

Friday, June 26. He looks awfully well considering he has been having undulant fever[65] and shingles but he has a nice new job and seems to fly to foreign places, which he loves. We talked all the morning and I did his washing and in the afternoon we went through the hives and he made another nucleus and helped me out of all my difficulties. He brought down the last remaining pair of canaries and put them in a disused chicken house where they can breed. We are to feed them on very little seed but heaps of green stuff and baked bread crumbs mixed with porridge oats. He had enough petrol for Father to take him back to Salisbury to catch the evening train to London, and he hopes to be down again quite soon. We always hope that – and then it is three months again.

Sunday, June 28. John and I went to tea with Ruth Grundy and met another mother there. They have such trouble with the sugar and butter rations and are all out by Sunday but the meat hangs fire very much as two of them do not eat any. They don't cook with sugar at all and neither do we, and that is how we manage to save some until stewed fruit begins again.

Monday, June 29. Mrs. Stuart sent me down a useful new booklet, *The A.B.C. of the W.V.S. Clothing Scheme*. It is just what we want and collects up all the letters we have had. It will be invaluable to Mother if she has to give anything out while I am away.[66] Father is rather disturbed by the news calling up of men up to 50. He says he may have to close the bottling stores and use those men in the main building.

---

64 Some 50 planes raided Poole in the early hours of June 4th. Details concerning the damage done are reported in Derek Beamish, Harold Bennett, and John Hillier, *Poole and World War II* (Poole Historical Trust, 1980), pp. 134–39.

65 An infection (brucellosis) which can result in chronic intermittent fever.

66 According to Lady Reading's foreword to this booklet, addressed to WVS workers, 'The work of the WVS Clothing Depots has become so much heavier and so much more complicated in the last few months, that I have felt for some time that we at Headquarters should try and help you by producing in an easily accessible form, all the information which we have circulated and which should be known to all responsible workers in Clothing Depots.' The booklet is found in the WRVS Archive, No. 821.

At this point there is an unexplained six-day gap in the diary.

Monday, July 6. Had a letter from the WVS about coupon free wool. There will be a new issue in September so applicants will only be allowed eight ounces until then and must produce their old clothing cards if possible. Mrs. R., our daily cook,[67] gave me her views on elementary schools in modern times. She has the job of cleaning them every evening and has done so for a long time. In the old days you only had to move a few long benches and there was no work in the sweeping and dusting but now there were countless little chairs and tables which took a long time and there was free milk spilt all over the floor and Nature Study meant the window sills cluttered up with little pots which upset if you looked at them, so that it was more like a day's work to get the place straight. Mrs. Ro. brought D. to tea. He goes to John's school and his father has just gone abroad. The child seems very delicate and has not played enough with other children. John behaved very badly but Mrs. Ro. was so glad to see someone else who had trouble with an only child. She seems to be one of those town people who have no idea of living in the country and only think of it in terms of the weekend cottage. Unfortunately D. got stung by a bee but we put soda on at once.

Tuesday, July 7. A Flag Day for the Dorset Comforts Fund. We always get about the same amount whatever we collect for, except the Red Cross, which is the most popular. Washed out my second-hand pram and cleaned it up for September. It seems quite a good bargain. Took John to have his hair cut. We had to wait a long time but it was quite well done. Went to the taxidermist to pay for having the horse mended which the children broke dropping cushions on our heads from the stairs as we came out from tea. They had only broken away from the board and needed a screw and she wanted to charge 7s 6d but I knew it was only because she thought I could afford it, so I said I thought it was excessive and after very little hooha she reduced it to 5s, which I paid. Picked and strung redcurrants in the evening, which my Mother bottled ready for the raspberries.

Wednesday, July 8. Long talk to Mrs. Oliver on the way back from school about petrol and getting the children there next term.[68] Mrs. F. is going to hire [a car] one day a week and will see them all there and Mrs. Oliver will do her two days as [usual] this term and the others as well if it is wet so it looks as if it will be quite easy even on the darkest mornings. Miss S., the stop gap teacher, says John has no visual idea of numbers and I must help him by playing a lot of games with them. She is going to lend me an easy book. Started on the clothing depot, stocktaking and putting this new moth stuff in the clothes. I must get it all foolproof so that Mother can work it easily when I am not here.

Thursday, July 9. Letters from India and Australia. Indian life seems to be going on as usual with plans for the hills in the hot weather. In Ceylon they are all set if the schools have to evacuate and they have been round to her about billeting Americans. She has no room to sleep them but has offered to feed several if they like. The children have been having swimming sports and J. won with breast stroke although all the children out there are taught the crawl at once. Her nurse, who is now in the WAAF

---

[67] Mrs Reed (information from John and Julian Walther).

[68] From the beginning of this month, petrol was not available for private use.

out there, had been home on leave very fit but suffering from the cold. They wondered, however, how she was going to manage if she was moved as they have to carry all their own kit and she had just bought herself an electric iron to add to everything else. Isabel had met a friend who had had awful experiences getting away from Singapore. They were torpedoed while she was bathing the children and only had time to snatch up their hats and their nightclothes. After some time in the boats they landed in Malaya and had to trek through the jungle. The youngest child got dysentery so badly that they had to be left behind in a mission where no one could speak a language they understood and they lived on rice for a time until the child was well enough to move back again to the coast and Australia. Went on moth hunting in the afternoon and gardened in the evening. Went round to an empty house whose garden has run to poppies and collect poppy heads for the canaries in the winter. Heard that the Cs' only son is missing from Tobruk.[69]

Friday, July 10. Finished the second-hand department of the clothing depot. Everything labelled and no moths. Mother had a communication about the meat pie scheme in rural areas. It does not come to much because we are so near the town and a British Restaurant. She rang up the outlying farmers and went and saw some others. If the Co-op could deliver them it would be the easiest thing. Only one lot of labourers will have them if they have to be fetched. Father went into Dorchester to a meeting of members of the Rural District Councils to hear about the Whitley Council scheme. On the way back his car broke down but he got a lift from someone else at the meeting. A cousin and his wife arrived from London.[70] He is the firm's lawyer and has come for the Board meeting. They had a house in Hampstead but when they could not get any servants they moved into a flat. They said all the flats in the block had filled up now since the last billeting census and the coal scheme. Heard again from Australia. Their chief trouble now is the clothing rationing, which has not come into force but the shops must only sell their quota which means that there is a queue at every draper's in the morning and nothing is left after they have been open a few hours, so that to get anything you have to down tools and join the queue. The schools have issued orders that each girl must have washable sanitary towels in case of evacuation and every mother was scrambling for Turkish towelling.

Saturday, July 11. Odd jobs all day and talking to Johnnie about life in London. They miss people dropping in for drinks so much and being cut off from all their friends. Shopping takes so long although there are no queues. So often the butcher or whoever it is has nothing at the time you go and you have to go again. They spend their points on meat things mostly. They had the dried cod but Johnnie said the smell had gone off by the time Ralph came back from the office. She found the beer the most difficult to get home as six bottles were so heavy to carry and then on Fridays the wine merchant let her have anything extra like whisky if he had it. Ralph and Father came back after a game of golf and we played croquet, which my John had got out.

Sunday, July 12. The Board lunch. The auditor could not arrive in time as he had been told a wrong bus that did not run on Sundays when he rang up the depot, so he

---

[69] Tobruk in Libya in North Africa, fell to Rommel on 21 June 1942.

[70] Ralph Woodhouse, first cousin to Phyllis and brother of Harold, below. He married Mabella Johnston, known in the family as 'Johnnie' (information from Julian Walther).

was stuck in Puddletown but managed to hitchhike from there and they had the meeting before dinner. Harold[71] told us that the Americans were going to take over the Camp and he would soon be out of a job. Ruth [Harold's wife] told us what she has to do as welfare officer of the ATS, one of those jobs which begins by spending a little money from some fund on curtains for their barracks and ends nowhere. She says she does not have to give advice in marriage troubles as the Army welfare officers do because the women seem to go to their officers whom they know while men prefer a civilian's advice. Their eldest son is at Marlborough and is going to Cambridge for a year to do Science before he joins up. They are so thankful he has not rushed off and will get on just as fast in the end.

Monday, July 13. Mother took Ralph and Johnnie and my John over to my sister's for tea so I washed my hair and picked some more poppy heads after having a nice morning sitting in the garden talking to Johnnie while the men played golf.

Tuesday, July 14. Mother bought a punnet[72] of cherries to bottle. It seems so lovely to be allowed a lot of anything. It is a pity they cannot reduce the price when there is such a glut of cherries. Went to the Killicks for tea. They have got a third doe now, a Flemish giant. Two got out and one never came back. Met Joan T. and heard her on the WVS. She finds it difficult to get up there as the buses are so full and short distance people are not allowed on. This makes it very difficult for Mrs. Stuart, who does not seem to appreciate the trouble. J.R. rang up to say he would come down tonight.

Wednesday, July 15. J.R. arrived at 2.30 in the afternoon having run out of petrol on the way with a headwind against him. He found he was running short in time to coast down all the hills and would have got through the town if a policeman had not held him up for an Army lorry so that he just had to push it over the bridge. He seems very well again and enjoying his job. Very keen on hospitality for American troops – and has been offered a job in connection with it – but he won't take it unless he has a military status and equivalent pay. He says it would be no good to try it as an attached civil servant. He used to get on very well indeed with the Americans who used to come over and stay at our hostel in the summer vacation but the rest of us found them most exhausting. Mother and Father are quite willing to entertain them if they don't expect to be fed. We went over to see Kathleen and Peter after supper. Her nannie is going for her holiday and having a month so is taking a job in a Priestley home[73] to help while their nurses have holidays. It will be interesting to hear what it is like. They had both been out over the weekend in Home Guard and invasion practices. Peter belongs to another Home Guard and had a quiet time sitting on a hill but Kathleen had been in the thick of it and giving first aid at a Rest Centre only to find she had made a mistake and should have stayed at home in what is to be the second First Aid station while her place is only at the Rest Centre when it is full of evacuees from other blitzed places.

---

[71] Harold Woodhouse, of West Lodge, Blandford, first cousin to Phyllis and brother of Ralph, above. He married Ruth Strange. Their eldest son was Edward. Col. H.S. Woodhouse was Officer Commanding the troops at Blandford Camp and Company Secretary at Hall and Woodhouse. He died of a heart attack during an air raid on the Camp in 1943 (information from Julian Walther).

[72] A small, light basket or container, used for soft fruit.

[73] We have been unable to find any more information about this.

Thursday, July 16. We did bees all day. The prospects for a honey crop seem rather more remote as the honey flow is supposed to end today.

Friday, July 17. Another day with the hives. J.R. went off after supper with some eggs, tomatoes and cucumbers.

Saturday, July 18. The Killicks came to tea. Her landlord is going to let her keep her rabbits in his sheds in the yard next to her cottage as long as she leaves him able to tie up a sick cow or something like that so they will be dry and snug in the wintertime.

Monday, July 20. Picked all the redcurrants and strung them with help from Mother and the evacuee. Picked raspberries in the afternoon as John had been asked to tea with his form mistress with the rest of his form and Mrs. Oliver was going down to help with the washing up so took him down with Ruth.

Tuesday, July 21. Finished off the clothing depot. It is now all boxed up with anti-moth stuff and a catalogue made and lists of where everything is so it ought to be easy to find anything as long as they do not suddenly dump a whole lot more on us. There has been a further outbreak of chickenpox in the school – three boys in John's form – so he will have to stay at home for a week longer. Went for a picnic with Ruth Grundy and the Killicks. Ruth swum and took the children in but they are not at all keen. Kathleen rang up in the evening and said she had been so low after her blood donation and had had to have a day in bed.

Wednesday, July 22. Turned out the nursery. Fetched the children from school. Richard Killick came to tea by himself and brought a fishing line but we had such trouble to find worms for bait and caught nothing in the end.

Thursday, July 23. Did needlework all the morning. School broke up. John announced that he had got a prize for trying so hard with his sums. Took some books into the town for a mile of Books for Salvage but they had not liked to risk laying the books out along the pavement so one just handed them in at the Corn Exchange, which seemed very dull. I do hope they look through them first because mine were really fit for the troops' library only. It was easier to leave them there than to go all the way to the post office.[74] Mother and Father went to the prize giving at the Grammar School as they are both Governors. The prizes were much fewer than in other years.

Friday, July 24. Planned going to Bournemouth with the Killicks for a day on the beach but Gay thought it was doubtful if we could go down as she had heard there were concentrations of barges at Weymouth and Poole and thought the beach would be closed everywhere. Decided to go on Monday if it was fine. Went to [Winterborne] Whitechurch for tea with Mrs. Keef to see the baby. She has a maid and works part-time in Dorchester for the Women's Land Army but it is very badly paid and the buses are so difficult that it takes all her money and time getting to work. They are

[74] 'It is the hope of salvage workers of Blandford that on the morning of Thursday, July 23rd residents . . . will be seen streaming towards the Marketplace, each carrying pile of unwanted books. At 10.30 a.m. the first book will be laid on the pavement outside the Town Hall, and it is hoped that by 6 p.m. there will be a mile long of books. It is estimated that at least 10,000 will be required.' (*Western Gazette*, 17 July 1942, p. 3.)

thankful to get someone who understands a job and can type. She says all the farmers on the coast have been told to evacuate their farms by August 10th so the invasion must really be going to take place. It does cheer one up. I had meant to take John to have his eyes tested by the man in Weymouth but now I think there will be raids and it is too dangerous and Bournemouth will do just as well. B. said that she had sweets sent from town where they were selling them off before rationing. We called in at our shop on our way home and got a half pound block of Fuller's everyday chocolate which she had saved for us. I told Father what I had heard and he called in at his shop and was given a pound tin of humbugs.

Saturday, July 25. Rang up an optical surgeon whose name was in the telephone directory and fixed an appointment for John for Wednesday as Ruth Grundy wants to go down with us one day. She came to tea with her stable companion who is the masseuse and looked after John for me. His feet are so much better from the exercises and massage that he can have sandals like the other boys at school and she gave me some limbering exercises for him and said he ought to learn to skip and needs physical training. The apples are getting ripe. It does seem lovely to have some again.

Monday, July 27. Rather a wet morning so we decided not to risk Bournemouth but I met J.T. in the town who had been down there on Saturday and said you could go down on the beach but they had stayed in the gardens. Decided to go down on Thursday, which makes two days running, but I expect I shall survive. Went to get John some sandals and had the greatest luck. They had ordered a pair for a girl whose feet had outgrown them by the time they arrived and they were just right for John and they can build them up a bit on the outside so they won't make his feet worse. Mother got some toilet soap with her coupons this month as we manage very well with the soap flakes ration. She could not get any of the kinds she wanted and the chemist told that he thought all soap would be standardised soon. We are very pleased about the extra allowance of treacle on points.

Tuesday, July 28. Letters from Australia. She had been to an American tea – a bring and buy sale in aid of the Red Cross. She had just got out of giving a talk on India as the president of the Society had died. She can't think why they are so keen on these little talks but supposed that no one had the time to read any travel books. Father came in saying they were going to have a Holidays at Home campaign in Poole Park and one of his publicans had been to implore him to provide extra beer for the canteens in the Park. It did not matter what it was like as long as it was something that would make for mateyness. They told him he was already having more than his quota but in the end they agreed to brew an extra 60,000 barrels of a special thin brew.[75] Mother and Father had a great treat and went down to the pictures by train to see *How Green is My Valley*. On paper the plan was ideal but the train was so late and

---

[75] In early August the Borough of Poole advertised its 'Holidays at Home Programme', which was to feature various recreational and sporting events running from August 6th to August 12th. 'The fun fair in Poole Park will be open every day. On Wednesday, August 12th, the entire proceeds will be given to the Lord Mayor's Empire Air Raid Distress Fund.' (*Poole and East Dorset Herald*, 6 August 1942, p. 4.) The objective was to discourage travel by train. Phyllis wrote 'we passed Poole Park in the train the other day and could see tents and marquees put up on the far side of the lake, but there was no notice about any goings-on at the station and I have not heard of anyone going to it from here.' (Directive Response, July 1942.)

there was no chance of a taxi so that 40 minutes of the big picture was over before they got in and they had to leave directly it was over to get the train back.

Wednesday, July 29. Went to Bournemouth by train with Ruth Grundy and John. It was a lovely day except just at lunchtime, which we planned to have on the beach, but it was all a mistake that one is allowed through the barbed wire and we sat on the promenade in a sea mist, but that cleared away in the end. John and I went off to see our man. We arrived at a very neglected house and rang the bell and eventually Dr. S. came. He was stone deaf and only has one leg but he seemed to know his job. The [place] was just like an antique shop with bits of glasses all over everything. I thought John would be too intimidated to say anything but he liked him in the end and I was glad to find out what was wrong. By the time we came away it was tea time so we had that with Ruth Grundy and then sat in the gardens until it was time to catch the train home. Rang up Gay Killick and told her about the beach being closed and decided to have a lunch picnic by the river here instead.

Thursday, July 30. The picnic was a great success and the children were very happy with boats, buckets and spades. I came home early because the gardener had promised to help get the supers off the hives. I gave [him] J.R.'s bee clothes in case of stings and I was glad I had because there were still a number of bees in the frames, and as it was he dropped one box but we put it on a tray and that will catch any honey which runs. He has picked in half a tree of plums as they are so loaded. The children loved them and Father is giving a lot away.

Friday, July 31. R. fetched the extractor for me and John and I spent the morning getting out the honey. I took the next lot in the evening. It is certainly much easier to do early in the season but it does not strain any faster. The Killicks came for a tea picnic. Her husband is getting a proper Bank Holiday weekend and his mother is coming over from Poole so she will be about the only person in the village with a house party. Mother went down to Hamworthy to see her brother who is working in munitions at 75.[76] He was in Southampton but knew he could not manage another winter in those digs and be so far from the work so he took a holiday and tried for work nearer home. He now works just across the road from his own bungalow and can come home to lunch. The work is almost too easy – just cutting out aeroplane parts from sheets of metal. The whole works are now having a week's holiday so she helped him with his garden and did mending. He gave some sugar he had saved.

[76] Frederick Witt (information from Julian Walther).

EPILOGUE

Phyllis Walther's diary ended with three more years of war still to be endured – and with much more war-related work still to be done in Blandford and nearby. Women continued to be central to these tasks on the home front, many of them organized by Women's Institutes and the Women's Voluntary Services.

The WVS continued to be active, and in January 1943 Lady Stavordale, the County Organizer, described the work done in and around Blandford. 'This Centre reports good attendance at Basic Training talks, but like every other rural district, describes the difficulties of organising these lectures with shortage of lecturers and transport. The Housewives' Service has started well. Twenty-four villages in this area now take part in the Pie Scheme. The WVS supply voluntary workers for serving meals in the British Restaurant: also breakfasts and suppers for workmen on the new camp. Much help is given to the local authorities with National Savings and Salvage. In one village a cart and horse collect the salvage, which is sorted out before being collected by the Rural District Council. Members of this Centre are still engaged in making and painting snipers' suits for the Home Guard.'[1] WVS monthly narrative reports for late 1942 and 1943 in the Blandford region mention a number of other ventures and contributions of women's labour, including a mobile library, YMCA canteens, mending socks for the troops, knitting for POWs and the merchant navy, supplying meat pies, organizing stirrup-pump teams to fight fires, book binding for naval libraries, and supplying jam for children's parties (partly courtesy of supplies from Canada).

Major changes were on the horizon with the appearance of American troops in large numbers, and local women turned their attention in various ways to the needs of the new arrivals. Americans in uniform soon became the beneficiaries of services provided by Dorset volunteers. One illustration came towards the end of the war from the Women's Institute in Winterborne Stickland. 'When wounded Americans lay languishing in the special hospital at Blandford, batches of iced cakes were made to cheer them and active needlewomen stitched calico bags to contain their treasured knick-knacks when they were flown home to America. Selected visitors sat by their bedsides to lighten the long drawn days of suffering.'[2]

Phyllis Walther lived for almost sixty years after writing the last words of her M-O diary. It is highly likely that the ending of her diary was closely linked to the arrival of her second child – Julian Walther was born on 21 September 1942 – for, with a new baby to care for, regular diary writing was probably not for her a priority. After 1942 she was (more or less) a single parent, now with two sons and her aging parents to care for. She saw her husband infrequently. The marriage, in fact, was unravelling – the

[1] WRVS Archive, Box 403, R6/3, Dorset, General Correspondence, Bulletin of January 1943. Snipers' suits were made from rough material painted in camouflage colours so that a sniper (a hidden marksman) could not be seen. Sometimes leaves and twigs were added.

[2] Dorset History Centre, W.19/1, Dorset Federation of Women's Institutes, War Record Book 1939–45, entry for Winterborne Stickland.

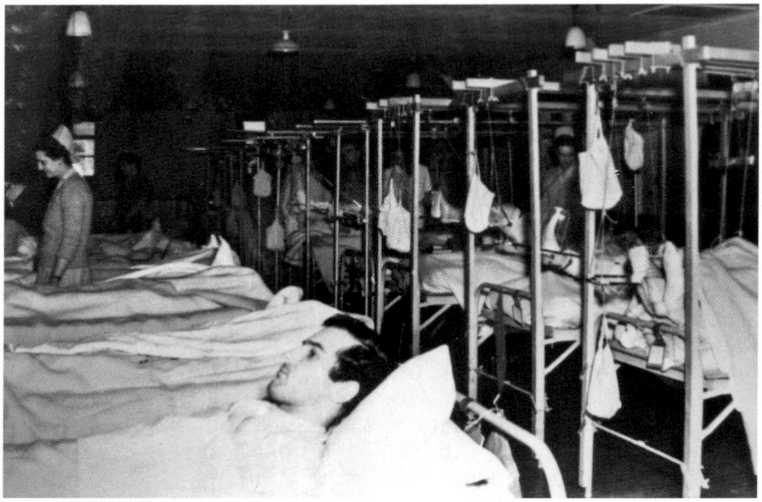

28. American soldiers in hospital at Blandford (note canvas bags hanging from their beds)

couple led largely separate lives from 1939 – though divorce proceedings were not pursued until around 1952/53, after the deaths of Phyllis's parents (she wanted to avoid causing them pain).

29. Phyllis in 1951

Phyllis then moved to Swanage, where she spent the rest of her life, working mostly in gardening and horticulture, about which she was passionate. She died on 22 February 2002, in her 98th year. In 2009 both her sons, John and Julian, were still living in Dorset and recalled their Mother fondly.

The publication of Phyllis Walther's diary allows us to appreciate more fully the realities of daily life for many women (and some men) in a part of wartime England that was not industrialized, though since it was close to the coast the sense of threat was ever-present. Her diary reveals in detail how one woman, in these extraordinary times, experienced motherhood, domestic responsibilities, personal privations, voluntary war work, friendship and duty. Above all, it shows how she and others helped the nation to cope, for the most part successfully, with challenges that had no precedent. Her diary is a record of experience that commands respect.

30. Phyllis with her Mother and Father after the war

31. Phyllis Walther in 1971

APPENDIX A

Blandford Forum in World War Two[1]

Blandford is a quiet country town in lovely Dorset, and if the war did not visit us in its more terrifying forms, we certainly did our bit to help our more unfortunate neighbours, and many were the lads in uniform that we hope we cheered on their way. As our W.I. Secretary in 1943 said 'We can safely say we have had a finger in most pies! Most certainly the W.I. is always called in to help tackle any job of business in the Town'.

In 1939 the W.I. was already hard at work in the Rest Room Canteen for the young Militiamen, cutting up 300 sandwiches, watching innumerable cakes disappear into what seemed to be 'bottomless pits'. The supply for the Canteen often failed and members had to supplement from their own larders! The Institute completed a busy year with canvassing for billets for evacuees and assembling gas masks. With the arrival of the evacuees came the setting up once monthly of the social afternoons for them and their children. Gathered together they talked, drank tea, aired their grievances with the W.I. members, who helped them with 'make-do-and-mend', while the children played.

During 1940, the Canteen kept W.I. members very busy as the B.E.F.[2] passed through, and the profits made were used to benefit the troops. At this time a letter was received from the father of a Birmingham soldier expressing his deep appreciation for the splendid work done by the W.I. Canteen helpers. A National Savings Group was started, and between seventy and eighty members and friends were hard at work knitting for the Army and Navy, and had already contributed four hundred and fifty garments to the County Comforts Fund. The A.R.P. Controller wrote thanking members for their speedy assistance in fixing filters to gas masks. Twelve stirrup pumps were presented to the town and a gift of £20 to the Spitfire Fund. A donation was also sent to the N.F.W.I.[3] Ambulance Fund which had given three ambulances to the country for the Army, Navy and Air Force. In the autumn, the members volunteered, at short notice, to canvas the town for fifty evacuees rendered homeless by air raids. Now Blandford saw many strange faces and among the many activities taken on by the ever ready W.I. was finding kind hearted people, willing for short periods to take in the wives and sweethearts of the many soldiers now in the town.

1941 opened with a party given for the evacuees by Mrs. Conyers, the President, and her helpers; also an Entertainment for Officers and Men stationed in the town held at the Corn Exchange. The admission was by invitation and our Mrs. Conyers, who was then combining the duties of Mayoress with W.I. President, acted as compére. It was

---

[1] This account was written shortly after 1945 and is reproduced here in full. (Dorset History Centre, W.19/1, Dorset Federation of Women's Institutes, War Record Book 1939–45.)

[2] British Expeditionary Force. See Glossary.

[3] National Federation of Women's Institutes.

32. Mayor Conyers launches Blandford Spitfire Fund in 1940

during this year that the W.I. lost one of its most active members, Mrs. W.J. Jeffries, Blandford's only woman A.R.P. Warden. She had been Secretary to both the W.I. and W.I. Canteen, and had been closely connected with the A.R.P. and W.V.S. and the local Billeting Committee. The Canteen still worked on becoming this year affiliated with the W.V.S. The Stall for vegetables came into being in the Shambles at the entrance to the Town Hall, to dispose of surplus garden produce once a week, staffed by the ever willing W.I. members, who were now digging out old batteries and helping with the new Ration Books. The end of the year brought a letter from the War Office, thanking the Canteen workers for their untiring efforts.

During 1942 the W.I. war time activities were reaching their peak, though they were not too busy to give thought and discussion to post-war reconstruction. To members came a personal message from the Mayor thanking them for the splendid help given to him in his year of office. Many and varied were the activities now – canteen, market stall, War Savings, knitting, organizing scheme for mending soldiers' socks, packing parcels for Blandford boys and girls in the Forces, and fire watching. The British Restaurant and the Rest Centre had its quota of W.I. helpers as did the salvage and camouflage net-making. This last will long linger in the memories of its helpers, as it was made up from horse hair and cowtails, smelling strongly of the farm yard and its late owners!

1944 repeated the activities of 1943 and so D. Day approached and the war drew to its victorious close. America came to Blandford, and with the U.S. soldiers came the American Red Cross Canteen. W.I. members packed parcels again for the boys overseas, and started knitting for the children of occupied countries. This year saw the retirement of the President of the W.I., Mrs. Conyers, who had held office for six years and had been indefatigable and untiring in her work during the war. In her last presidential report, she hoped that the W.I. would maintain the reputation they had made in the war years.

In 1945 the W.I. Canteen closed, after being open without a break since 1939. It had made a name for pleasant service, and dispensed good cheer as well as sustenance to thousands of soldiers. The many letters received from the boys dispersed all over the fighting fronts pays the finest possible tribute. And so the war years ended, with a feeling of work well done by all members of the Blandford W.I.

I have only been able to give a bare framework; there must be many situations, amusing and otherwise, many anecdotes that will never be told. A book would be needed to tell of all the happenings, the people that came and went during the war.

One name only is mentioned, that of Mrs. J. Conyers, who stands for all W.I. members who worked so hard to help their country in their own way. Blandford W.I. is proud to stand with the ranks of the many who fought for peace.

Local Invasion Committee

A Local Invasion Committee has been set up in order to deal with invasion conditions.

DURING THE PRESENT PERIOD the Committee is engaged in making preparations to deal with the local problems which will arise in invasion such as :—

1. Organisation of civilian labour to assist the military in preparing defence works, digging trenches, clearing roads, etc.
2. Care of wounded.
3. Housing and sheltering the homeless.
4. Emergency cooking and feeding.
5. Emergency water supplies.
6. Messenger Service.

IF INVASION COMES the Committee will direct its action :

(*a*) to meet the requirements of the military,
(*b*) to attend to the needs of the civil population.

All civilians both men and women must be prepared to play their part.

Give in your name now to the Committee's Headquarters, or through your Warden or the W.V.S. Housewives' Service, for the work for which you are best fitted. The Committee will see that you are allotted a task, and if necessary trained to carry it out.

OFFER YOUR SERVICES NOW.

If Invasion comes the Committee instructs everyone

NOT to spread rumours,

NOT to block roads by becoming a refugee,

but

To follow the orders of the Police, A.R.P., Military and Home Guard,

TO STAND FIRM.

The composition of the Committee and its Headquarters are :—

MR. W. H. WILSON *(Chairman)*
MR. A. J. E. BLANDFORD
MR. J. E. CONYERS
MR. B. C. HUNT

THE SENIOR MILITARY OFFICER
THE SENIOR HOME GUARD OFFICER
THE SENIOR POLICE OFFICER
THE A.R.P. DISTRICT CONTROLLER
THE MEDICAL OFFICER OF HEALTH
THE SENIOR NATIONAL FIRE SERVICE OFFICER
THE FOOD EXECUTIVE OFFICER

Headquarters :— The Red House, 75, Salisbury Street, Blandford.

15th August, 1942.

APPENDIX B

Bryanston in World War Two[1]

Bryanston enjoys the doubtful privilege of being situated in the heart of a private estate. The 'Big house' is now a public school for boys. The nearest high road being two miles away, it was therefore the ideal training ground for troops, and early in the war we had militia billeted in what was once the hunting stables.

After Dunkirk, the many trees around the village made a good hiding place for the Royal Artillery. Every suitable bit of ground had its canvas tent, every tree its gun or tractor, affectionately called by every villager a 'Quad', under its camouflage netting. Homecoming from the cinema amongst the dark trees, a frightening voice would hail 'Who goes there?' and we'd see the gleam of a bayonet pointing threateningly at us, show our Identity Cards, and be allowed to enter our garden gates. We got used to it after a while and felt slighted if for some reason we weren't stopped.

Away went the Royal Artillery, folding their tents like the Arabs and silently stole away, but not so silently that we didn't miss them for the quiet of our daily life seemed even quieter. But not for long. Soon after a Company of Royal Engineers descended with lorry loads of building materials. They cut trees, cleansed the site of undergrowth, and in a few short weeks Nissen huts, cook houses, storerooms, guard room and all the usual offices sprang up around us. Roads were widened, new roads made, trees festooned with telephone and electric cables, and we felt that at last Bryanston had become important. We were a military camp. But we would gaze enviously at the brilliantly lighted living quarters, thinking of our paraffin oil lamps indoors.

From then onwards a procession of regiments were in occupation – reconnaissance, searchlight and balloon section, Royal Signal Corps, more artillery, big anti-aircraft guns, little four-pounders, and Bailey bridge companies[2] – a veritable paradise for our small boy collectors of cap-badges, shoulder-flashes, and numerals.

The Women's Institute opened a canteen in a room that had once been a laundry, having to overflow into a neighbouring cart shed if extra troops came through on an exercise or similar manoeuvres. Entertainments in the way of concerts and dances were organized in the school gymnasium. But the canteen was discontinued on the arrival of coloured troops from the USA who brought their own arrangements. The village was thrilled. Opinion divided as to whether they should be called Blackies, Niggers, or Darkies. 'Old Ephraim', who in his younger days belonged to a black-faced minstrel show, was heard to remark 'And to think I used to black my face wi' a bit o' burnt

---

[1] Bryanston is just west of Blandford Forum. Some of the language used in describing black American soldiers would not be acceptable today. This account of its wartime history was written shortly after 1945, and is reproduced here in full. (Dorset History Centre, W.19/1, Dorset Federation of Women's Institutes, War Record Book 1939–45.)

[2] A Bailey bridge was made of lattice steel and designed to be assembled quickly from prefabricated parts.

cark'. Hearing them speak took our thoughts immediately to 'The Swanee Ribber' and 'De Old Folks at Home'.

Afterwards came the white Yanks with everything on wheels, tailor shops, boot repair, all-electric mobile workshops, anti-aircraft guns and locators, and the weirdest looking machines blocking our narrow roads, practising and rehearsing for 'D-day'. The Americans made their mark on our countryside. Hardly a tree but has its bark carved with one or more names and addresses from outlandish towns like Cleveland, Ohio, Texas, and Oregon.

In common with other villages, Bryanston had its Red Cross working party and a tremendous amount of knitted garments were made for troops and relief of the children of Europe.[3] Pull-throughs for Army rifles were manufactured, salvage collected, comfort parcels sent to boys and girls who were serving. We supplied a few members of Blandford Home Guard Company, had our own special constable, ARP wardens, First Aid, and rescue squads, complete with stretcher, gas rattle, and stirrup pump.

Although many German aeroplanes passed over our parish on their way to Bristol, few bombs were dropped and our only damage – and this of unknown origin – was a bullet which entered the church vestry window and buried itself in an oak door frame, passing through twelve folds of curtain in its flight. Five small bombs fell, did not explode and so did no damage except large holes in the school playing fields.

Bryanston sent 70 boys and girls into all branches of the Forces. Three gave their lives for their country. Our population in those days was 220.

Such is the short record of war years in this quiet little village in Dorset.

[3] It was common to provide such relief for the Continent at and just after the end of the war.

APPENDIX C

Winston Churchill

While Phyllis never mentions Winston Churchill in her diary, she does discuss him in her Directive Responses, in answer to a question about his leadership.

I think we are all agreed that he is the only possible leader because he is the strongest man we have. He is typically English and knows what he wants and can stand up to leaders in any other country and we know he will do his best. I deplore his attitudes to India in the past and I don't think he has the least understanding of workers' minds. He never seems to read any criticism or act on it and he must go directly the war is over or we shall have the most glorious mess for our children to clean up. He is too old really. It does not seem possible to get the confidence and experience of the older man and the hope in the future of the young. The England he thought so glorious is gone forever but he cannot think of the fresh glories we have faith and hope in. (*March, 1942.*)

A month later, when replying to a question about the wartime political truce, she mentioned Churchill again.

I wish that Churchill had not remained a party man and we did not have to think of him as a diehard Conservative, which he has not been always, and I wish that the Labour members of the Government appeared at least as party conscious as the Conservatives. *(April, 1942.)*

GLOSSARY

A.R.P. The Air Raid Precautions Act of 1937 allowed for the building of shelters, the issuing of gas masks, planning for blackout, and training of wardens. ARP wardens were responsible for ensuring the blackout was maintained, constructing air-raid shelters, and co-ordinating rescue services in the event of an enemy attack. Each warden had an area assigned to him or her.

A.T.S. Auxiliary Territorial Service. A reserve force of trained women founded in 1917, it was disbanded in 1921 but re-established in 1938. In 1941 the National Service Act allowed the conscription of women, and many joined the A.T.S. They were formed into separate all-female units and worked as telephonists, drivers, mess orderlies, postal workers, inspectors of munitions and on anti-aircraft batteries.

Auxiliary Fire Service. Formed in 1937 of volunteers, they undertook nightly fire-watching duties, informing the emergency services of fires caused by incendiary bombs and also of approaching enemy aircraft. They worked with the other emergency services in dealing with the aftermath of bombing raids.

Blackout. Householders were instructed to cover all windows at night so that no chink of light escaped. Special thick black material could be bought for this. Vehicle lights had to be dimmed and only project downwards. Streetlights were fitted with a special screen to dim the light, or they were turned off. These measures were designed to make it difficult for enemy aircraft to sight their targets during night bombing raids.

Blandford Camp. Blandford Camp, two miles north-east of Blandford Forum, was at this time a major Army combat training camp. From 1944 it served as a U.S. Army Hospital.

Board of Trade. Established as a Committee of the Privy Council in 1621 to oversee the economic life of the country, by the twentieth century it also dealt with company regulation, labour and factory matters, patents, and contracts between government and industry.

British Expeditionary Force. Formed in the First World War to fight in Europe, the B.E.F. was deployed across the Channel early in the Second World War. In May of 1940 the Germans forced them back to the coast, and they were evacuated from Dunkirk in a hastily organized flotilla of boats.

British Restaurant. Non-profit, cafeteria-style restaurants where food could be purchased ‘off-ration’ (i.e., without surrendering coupons) were set up by local authorities throughout the nation from the beginning of 1941. The name ‘British Restaurant’ was suggested by Winston Churchill himself as preferable to the name ‘Communal Feeding Centre’.

Buttercup Days. Flag days in aid of Orthopaedic Hospitals for Crippled Children. They were established in the 1920s or earlier.

Central Hospital Supply Service. Run jointly by the Red Cross and St. John's Ambulance to supply their hospitals with essential bedding, towels, pyjamas and bandages for the care of wounded military personnel.

Church of England's Children's Society. Founded in 1881, it provided for the welfare of orphaned or abandoned children throughout England and Wales. Its official title was the Church of England Incorporated Society for Providing Homes for Waifs and Strays. In 1946 it was renamed the Church of England's Children's Society and in 1982 it became The Children's Society. It is still in operation.

Communal Feeding Centre. See British Restaurant.

Conscription. See National Service.

Daylight saving. First introduced in Britain in May 1916, when the clocks were advanced by one hour in the summer, it was retained through the inter-war years. During the Second World War, double summer time (two hours in advance) was introduced. This meant that the clocks were two hours ahead in summer and one hour in winter.

District Nursing Association. Before the National Health Service was set up in 1948, local Associations provided nursing to the community. Members paid an annual subscription. Nursing was provided by trained staff and usually included midwifery.

Fire watching. Manned by volunteers, the Fire Guard spent their nights on rooftops and high points watching for bombs and incendiary devices, and trying to put out the fires they caused.

Holidays at Home. In 1941 the government, recognizing that people needed to have a rest from the rigours of wartime daily life and, to keep up their spirits, encouraged them to take holidays. Because of the pressures on public transport, people were discouraged from travelling and instead take their Holidays at Home. Entertainment was put on in public parks and sponsored catering was provided. Despite the overcrowding on trains and buses, many people did get away to beauty spots, although wartime restrictions meant that many seaside resorts were not operating as normal.

Home Guard. In May 1940 Anthony Eden called for male civilians aged 16–65 (although some were older in practice) to join the Local Defence Volunteers. Churchill renamed it the Home Guard in July 1940. Formed to defend the country from invasion and to protect vital installations, it was a voluntary corps consisting mainly of men too old to join up, young men waiting until they were old enough to enlist, and those in reserved occupations. Under the National Service (Number 2) Act of December 1941, males could be called up for service in the Home Guard.

Infant Welfare. This was 'the maternity and child welfare centre where mothers could get advice on the ordinary day-to-day questions of their babies' feeding and general care. The clinics were run by local authorities or voluntary organizations and were staffed by health visitors and voluntary workers, and a doctor was usually in attendance. Mothers were encouraged by the health visitors to take their children to the centres for regular examination. Furthermore, most of the centres tried to attract the mothers by maintaining a friendly social atmosphere.' (Sheila Ferguson and Hilde Fitzgerald, *Studies in the Social Services* [London: H.M.S.O., 1954], p. 146.)

Land Girls. See Women's Land Army.

Lord Mayor's National Air Raid Distress Fund. Its purpose was to aid people whose property was damaged or destroyed by enemy bombing, and this aid might take the form of new or used clothes, grants to help restart businesses, supplementary payments for lost housing, and grants for the education of children who had lost a parent. The W.V.S. acted for the Fund with regard to the supply of clothing. (*The Lord Mayor's National Air Raid Distress Fund* [1946], especially p. 78, a pamphlet held in the Guildhall Library, London.)

Ministry of Food. Set up in 1938 (formerly part of the Board of Trade). It was responsible for the control, supply and distribution of all types of food (including milk, cereals and meat) and for issuing ration books.

Ministry of Information. Set up on 4 September 1939 (the day after war broke out), this department was responsible for publicity and propaganda. The aim was to maintain public morale and counter enemy propaganda. Brendan Bracken was minister from April 1941 almost to the end of the war.

Ministry of Labour. Established in 1916, it took on some of the work previously covered by the Board of Trade. In 1939 the title was changed to Ministry of Labour and National Service and a new Military Recruitment Department dealt with National Service, conscientious objection and re-settlement and civil employment after demobilization. In 1941 it also took on responsibility for National Service Hostels, set up by the minister, Ernest Bevin, to provide accommodation for workers employed in munitions and other essential wartime occupations.

Ministry of Supply. Set up in June 1939 to address the problem of essential supplies in wartime. Orders for the control of strategic materials, such as petrol and steel, followed. Scrap metal came under this heading, including the seizure of iron railings and the collection of household utensils.

Moral and Spiritual Welfare. A voluntary organization concerned with the welfare of unmarried pregnant women and unmarried mothers, it often had a strict disciplinary approach.

Motor Transport Service. There were many varieties of Motor Transport Services. The Home Guard set up their own local services, the Army used the Auxiliary Territorial Service (women), and other voluntary units sprang up.

N.A.A.F.I. Navy, Army and Air Force Institutes. Founded in 1921, they sold goods to servicemen and their families and ran recreational establishments for the forces.

National Milk Scheme. Set up in April 1940, it gave every child under five and every expectant mother one pint of cut-price milk every day.

National Savings. Begun in 1916 during the First World War, it continued in the inter-war period with local and regional committees. A new seventh issue of National Savings Certificates was issued in the Second World War and saving was strongly urged as a patriotic gesture. Each certificate cost 15 shillings and promised to pay 20s 6d after ten years. Many people saved by buying a National Savings stamp for 6d and sticking it on a printed card, to be exchanged for a Certificate when the card was full. Savings Clubs were established, with volunteers going round to collect from subscribers.

National Service. In 1939 the National Service (Armed Forces) Act made men aged between 18 and 41 liable for conscription into the armed forces. In 1942 a government directive ordered that all people should be interviewed and registered for National Service on reaching the age of 16, after which they would wait to be 'called up' unless they were unfit or in a reserved occupation. Eventually all men between 18 and 50 were required to register for national service. In December 1941 the National Service Act introduced conscription for single women and widows between 20 and 30 without children. The age limit was later expanded to include women between 19 and 43. See H.M.D. Parker, *Manpower: A Study of Wartime Policy and Administration* (London: H.M.S.O., 1957), Table VII, p. 491.

Personal Service League. Set up in the 1930s as a voluntary organization (mainly of well-to-do women) to supply clothes for unemployed men and their families. Their work was expanded on the outbreak of war.

Public Assistance Board. Public Assistance Committees, successors to the Poor Law, were established by statute in 1929. They provided means-tested relief for the destitute and those in distress, including the elderly, children, and the poor and disabled. These committees and their officers exercised considerable discretion in determining the scale and conditions of the relief given.

Rationing. Started officially in January 1940, although there were shortages before then. Rationing started with butter, sugar and bacon but soon extended to include many other basic foodstuffs, clothes and household items. Prices were strictly controlled. Imported items were scarce because of the German blockade of shipping and home production was scaled down as factories turned over to producing war material. A ration book and clothing coupons were issued to each civilian and shops advertised the number of coupons required as well as the prices on their goods. Petrol was rationed from 1939 and from mid-1942 only issued to those on official business.

Red Cross. Formed individually in several countries during the latter part of the 19th century, the League of Red Cross Societies (which included Britain) was founded in 1919 to give relief assistance in wartime and emergency situations. In World War Two, Red Cross volunteers worked alongside the W.V.S., A.R.P., and the emergency services. The Red Cross is still an active international body.

Rest Centres. Rest Centres were intended to accommodate, temporarily, people whose homes had been destroyed. There were eleven Rest Centres in Blandford.

Rosehips. The difficulty of importing fruit meant that another source of Vitamin C was needed. In 1941 the Vegetable Drugs Committee of the Ministry of Health and the Ministry of Supply appealed for rosehips, growing wild in hedgerows, to be collected. The collections were often organized by the W.I. and the W.V.S. The rosehips were made into syrup, which was distributed to children over five years (the younger ones were receiving orange juice). Collectors were paid 3d per pound. The National Rosehip Scheme carried on into the 1950s.

Royal Army Service Corps. These were drivers, mainly of lorries, who transported supplies of arms, ammunition, food, tents and clothing for the military.

Royal Corps of Signals. Responsible for installation and maintenance of communication links for the Army.

Salvage schemes. The W.V.S. was responsible for organizing the collection of waste paper for pulping to make new paper, and later aluminium pots and kitchen utensils and other metals for melting down and making into armaments. Both of these raw materials were in short supply.

Signals Corps. See Royal Corps of Signals.

Soldiers', Sailors' and Airmen's Families Association. Provided aid to the spouses of men serving in the Forces.

Southern Command. After the evacuation at Dunkirk in 1940, the U.K. forces were put under the control of G.H.Q. Home Forces. The whole of the U.K. was divided into military commands in preparation for possible invasion. Dorset was in the Southern Command.

V.A.D. Voluntary Aid Detachment. A scheme to provide nursing for sick and wounded servicemen, run jointly by the Red Cross and St John's Ambulance. It was set up in 1909 and continued throughout both World Wars. Some nurses worked in the field, others in hospitals which were often set up in large houses given over by their owners during the war.

Waifs and Strays. See Church of England Children's Society.

War Agricultural Executive Committee. Set up in 1939 on the outbreak of war. Their job was to maximise food production from the land. They controlled the way land was farmed, administered grant and subsidy schemes, assisted with the provision of modern machinery and oversaw the rationing of animal feed and fertilisers. They also employed labour (including the Women's Land Army) to clear land for production.

Warships Week. Organized by the National War Savings Committee, these events encouraged people to donate towards the cost of building a specific ship.

Whitley Council. A council for relations between the employers and the employees, named after the author of the Report for the Civil Service by John Henry Whitley in 1918. It dealt with conditions of service and grievances, and later advocated national pay scales. In 1941 the Association of County Councils began to consider establishing a Whitley Council scheme for Local Government authorities. Uniform national salary scales and conditions of employment for Local Government employees were agreed in 1946. The scheme is still in operation.

W.A.A.F. Women's Auxiliary Air Force, formed in 1939. The women served as individual members of R.A.F commands. They worked as mechanics and fitters, in the radar establishments, as plotters, as telegraphists and with codes and ciphers. In December 1941 the National Service Act introduced the conscription of women and many joined the W.A.A.F.

Welfare. See Infant Welfare.

Women's Institute. Founded in Canada in 1897, the first British meeting was in 1915. It had two aims: the revitalisation of rural communities and the encouragement of women to be involved with food production during World War One. In the 1930s the movement expanded both in numbers and in activities, combining social events (meetings, plays, concerts) with campaigning on issues such as water supply to villages, equal pay for women and men, and alleviating the distress caused by unemployment. When war broke out in 1939, the W.I. was closely involved in overseeing the mass evacuation of children from cities. Their observation of the health and living conditions of city children led to their report 'Town Children through Country Eyes' (1941), which pressed for a national child allowance and nursery provision among other things. In 1940 the W.I. was asked by the Ministry of Food to run the Fruit Preservation Scheme. They purchased £1,400 worth of sugar which was distributed to the Federations. In 1940 alone 1,631 tons of fruit was preserved. As the war progressed the W.I. helped dispense cod liver oil and fruit juice under government schemes, assisted with the delivery of school meals in rural areas, gave food advice (how to provide a balanced diet, how to make rations go further) and promoted schemes for home breeding of rabbits, poultry, pigs and growing vegetables. They were also involved in the repair of rubber boots for agricultural workers. Their canteens catered for evacuees and the services (A.T.S, W.A.A.F., Land Army, Home Guard), to whom they also provided welfare. The W.I. is still in operation.

Women's Land Army. First formed in 1917 in response to the shortage of farm labourers, it was disbanded in 1919 but re-established in 1939 by Lady Denman. At first the movement relied on volunteers, who were employed directly by farmers or by the local War Agricultural Executive Committee. In December 1941 the National Service Act introduced conscription for females and allowed women to join the W.L.A as their national service, which brought in many more members. The women were paid rates set down by the Board of Agriculture, but these varied according to their employer.

W.V.S. The full title of W.V.S during the war was 'Women's Voluntary Services for Civil Defence'. Formed in 1939 under the determined and energetic Lady Reading, they were first involved with evacuation from the cities and subsequently ran Rest Centres, organized facilities for people made homeless by bombing, ran mobile canteens for people in the emergency services and organized welfare services for troops. The women also helped run Communal Feeding Centres or British Restaurants, organised salvage drives and clothing supplies, and were responsible for the home production of knitted and hand-sewn garments for the forces and for V.A.D hospitals. The work was voluntary and most W.V.S members were unpaid. There may have been as many as 400 women in various W.V.S work parties in Blandford and the surrounding region in 1941–42, plus around 20 at the Centre, of which Phyllis Walther was one. The Monthly Narrative Reports from Blandford are held in the W.R.V.S Archive & Heritage Collection at Steventon, Abingdon, Oxfordshire. The name was changed in 1966 to Women's Royal Voluntary Service – W.R.V.S, under which it operates now.

Y.M.C.A. Young Men's Christian Association. Founded in 1844 as a non-denominational Christian movement to help young people, it evolved to provide education, training and recreation and hostels for the homeless. During World War Two the organization provided troops with food and drink and writing paper and envelopes, as well as running mobile canteens for bomb victims and emergency service workers. It is still in operation. The Y.W.C.A provides assistance to women.

Index

Page numbers in *italics* denote illustrations. The letter 'n' following a page number indicates that the reference will be found in a footnote.